LEAVE SOMETHING ON THE TABLE

AND OTHER SURPRISING LESSONS FOR
SUCCESS IN BUSINESS AND IN LIFE

FRANK BENNACK

SIMON & SCHUSTER

NEW YORK   LONDON   TORONTO   SYDNEY   NEW DELHI

Simon & Schuster
1230 Avenue of the Americas
New York, NY 10020

First Simon & Schuster hardcover edition October 2019

SIMON & SCHUSTER and colophon are registered trademarks of Simon & Schuster, Inc.

For information about special discounts for bulk purchases, please contact Simon & Schuster Special Sales at 1-866-506-1949 or business@simonandschuster.com.

The Simon & Schuster Speakers Bureau can bring authors to your live event. For more information or to book an event contact the Simon & Schuster Speakers Bureau at 1-866-248-3049 or visit our website at www.simonspeakers.com.

Interior design by Carly Loman

Manufactured in the United States of America

10   9   8   7   6   5   4   3   2   1

Library of Congress Cataloging-in-Publication Data
Names: Bennack, Frank A., author.
Title: Leave something on the table : and other surprising lessons for success in
    business and in life / Frank Bennack.
Description: New York : Simon & Schuster, 2019. | Includes index.
Identifiers: LCCN 2019027888 (print) | LCCN 2019027889 (ebook) |
    ISBN 9781982114152 (hardcover) | ISBN 9781982114176 (ebook)
Subjects: LCSH: Bennack, Frank A. | Publishers and publishing—United States—
    Biography. | Success in business. | Success.
Classification: LCC Z473.B424 A3 2019 (print) | LCC Z473.B424 (ebook) |
    DDC 070.5092 [B]—dc23
LC record available at https://lccn.loc.gov/2019027888
LC ebook record available at https://lccn.loc.gov/2019027889

ISBN 978-1-9821-1415-2
ISBN 978-1-9821-1417-6 (ebook)

I dedicate this book about my life and about Hearst, the company where I spent most of my life, to our eight children, fifteen grandchildren, and five great-grandchildren. It is my fond hope that they will be pleased with what I was up to during the countless hours I was out of their sight.

Contents

Prologue

This is a book of stories. I was CEO of Hearst for almost three decades, so many of those stories are about business. But the point of telling these stories is not to revisit old challenges, brag about long-ago successes, or explain how, on my watch, we transformed a 1950s magazine and newspaper company into a hundred-year-old start-up.

Although I'm in many of these stories—hey, it's my book—they're really about the people in my life, and what I learned from them, and what we accomplished together.

In many of these stories you'll also meet two remarkable and accomplished women. Luella Mae Smith, my high school girlfriend, became my wife for more than fifty years. She died tragically and without warning on April 17, 2003. She is central to the period from 1949 to 2003. Dr. Mary Lake Polan, to whom I was married on April 2, 2005, has supported me and enriched my life on many levels. She has been an important force throughout my second tour as CEO of Hearst, as well as during my Lincoln Center and NewYork-Presbyterian Hospital chairmanships. Like Luella, she has made the good times better and the difficult times bearable.

If these stories offer some wisdom, it's this: the importance of values in our private lives and work lives—the value of values.

You don't hear much about values in the business press these days. Mostly you hear about transactions. That's inevitable. The deals are bigger now. There's more and louder publicity accompanying them. The claimed benefits generally include a better world—often a better world through technology.

Some of the stories you'll find in these pages describe transactions that made headlines, but what's more important, I think, is how and why those transactions happened. Underpinning the business reasons were relationships, some going back for decades. And underpinning those relationships was mutual understanding. It didn't need to be verbalized—our lives and our businesses were the proof. Under our roofs, people came together, shared a mission, created a culture, and produced superior products. And what connected them? Our shared values.

This will sound quaint to some readers.

Institutional culture and character—building it, maintaining it, passing it on—is a slow process. My parents taught me what is important—honesty, integrity, hard work, concern for others—and that mistakes, and I've made my share, can be overcome. My mentors showed me how to build on that foundation. My colleagues and partners led by example. And then our enterprise succeeded beyond our expectations.

We live in a time of the instant trend, the pop-up shop, the product that defines the moment and vaporizes fast. Of course, there are businesses that have experienced meteoric growth because they were first with a good idea; Hearst invested in some and got a nice return. But others puzzle me. How can enormously profitable companies take no responsibility for what appears on their screens? If a company becomes successful by running rough-shod over the competition and flaunting its ability to operate out-side government regulations, can it really reform itself? And this, most of all: Can a company that runs on algorithms ever acquire human values?

It's not currently fashionable to make the case for the high road. It looks longer, and old-fashioned, and it's easy to conclude that while you're climbing the ladder, burdened by your values, others are reaching the top faster. But if the stories in these pages suggest a broader truth, it's exactly the opposite: The high road is quicker, with a better view along the way, and more satisfaction at the summit. And you end up loving rather than hating your partners.

I've worked for Hearst for more than six decades. I was its leader for twenty-eight years. That makes me a double unicorn—in this century, few will collect gold watches for long service, and fewer will lead businesses for decades. But it's not just CEOs who are confronting an uncertain future. In this supercharged climate, solid achievement and energetic commitment are no guarantee of continued success; everyone, at every level, in every enterprise, is legitimately anxious. So how are smart, ambitious people to make their way?

I believe there is one unchanging North Star. It isn't what you know, and how hard you work, and how clever you are. It's not even who you know. It's how other people know you. It's who you are.

LEAVE
SOMETHING
ON THE TABLE

CHAPTER 1

As Soon as You're Old Enough to Work . . . Get a Job

My mother had just two rules for her only child, but they sufficed. One: Comb your hair. Two: As soon as you're able to work, you've got to get a job. So, hair neatly combed, I started working when I was eight. I earned a dollar a day helping a neighborhood couple cater Mexican food at Camp Bullis, a World War II–era military base north of San Antonio. Then I invested that dollar in vegetable and flower seeds that I sold door-to-door.

I sold seeds until I was eleven, old enough for Doc Thompson, our neighborhood pharmacist, to give me a job delivering prescriptions, ultimately promoting me to soda jerk. In that job, my biggest joy was bringing home quarts of Lady Borden vanilla ice cream for my family to enjoy. I also often treated a neighborhood girl or two to ice cream sodas or milkshakes. When payday rolled around, I had usually charged so much that my remaining salary could be paid in coins. I graduated to a paper route after I reached high school. In a stroke of what seems like fate, the paper I was delivering would be my competitor years later.

Whenever Mom felt I wasn't working hard enough, she threatened to charge me rent. She never followed up.

♦

My mother's family was Old Texas. Her father, Nolton Max Connally, was the brother of the father of John Connally, the Texas governor, secretary of the navy, and secretary of the treasury. My mom, Lula Wardell Connally, was the fourth of nine surviving children of Nolton and Elisabeth Connally. Mom's official name was Louisiana. Her older sister was named Nevada. I always wondered what my grandparents had in mind when they started naming children after states.

Like her brothers and her Connally cousins, Mom was a born leader, and she led our family even though she was sick during my entire childhood. And not with one disease—she had gall bladder surgery, thyroid surgery, and several bouts of double pneumonia during a period when pneumonia was especially perilous. Every time she went to the hospital, I was afraid she was never coming back. Sometimes my family had a car; other times, after one of Mom's hospitalizations, it had to be sold.

My elementary school days were uneven because St. Gerard's, the Catholic school that my parents wanted me to attend, required a modest tuition they couldn't always pay. So I went to Fannin Public School in the first grade (I had Mrs. Butler, the same first grade teacher my dad had) and to St. Gerard's in the second grade. Back to Fannin for third through sixth, then St. Gerard's again in the seventh and eighth.

I never felt poor, though at times I guess we were. I really didn't think much about the fact that country sausage links, my dad's favorite, or a chuck roast on Sunday represented a special treat. We ate Swiss chard and turnips from our own garden. Asparagus was often a main course. Frequently we ate canned pork and beans or salmon patties made from canned salmon, a dish I still love. I never minded coloring the margarine to make it look like real butter. And I don't recall ever being hungry.

My mother's brother had a hog farm, and fattened his hogs for market by feeding them the food garbage he picked up daily from local restaurants. The cans and bags of food waste invariably also contained kitchen utensils thrown out by careless restaurant workers; my uncle provided us with knives, forks, and spoons. After I got married I reveled in the fact that every knife matched every other knife.

My clothes mostly were donations from a thoughtful neighborhood lady. She took care of the child of the "wealthy" local undertaker and was able to pass along to me that child's hand-me-downs, often frayed and shiny from wear. My clothes didn't make me feel poor. But I did hate to wear short pants.

As for an actual money shortage, I guess I thought my dad's monthly pleading at the front door with our landlord about needing more time to pay the rent on our three-room frame house was what every dad had to do.

If I never felt underprivileged, it was mostly because I was anxious almost every day about something else: my mother's unending illnesses. But I give my parents great credit here. They did what they could to shield me from my mother's health problems, and that, in combination with their unreserved love, kept me a happy and fulfilled kid. I've observed from my own children, and especially from my grandchildren, that even at an early age they absorb more than we suspect. At age four or five it's unlikely that I intellectually understood the lesson my parents were demonstrating: In times of adversity, never give up. But I believe I instinctually grasped that lesson. There's no more powerful message; it creates optimism, even in difficult times, and optimism, as we know, can be a contagious force.

◆

My father, Frank A. Bennack Sr., was the biggest single influence on my values and work ethic. After struggling through the Great Depression, most of his working life was spent as a letter carrier for the United States Postal Service. His life's passion, however, was the arts, performing and visual. Although he never got a chance to earn his living that way, he exposed me to his passion for the arts in a way that I never forgot.

Through late-night homework assistance and school project support sessions, he taught me that it's important to do what you are supposed to do and do it well. Just as important were the countless narratives about his life and the lessons he had learned: who was good and who was evil, which values endured and which were fads. Early on it was clear that he believed his only son— my parents had a baby before me, but he died at or shortly after birth—had the ability to accomplish almost anything. By the time I was twelve, my father had very consciously begun treating me as an adult, and, through me, lived the life that hadn't been possible for him, a paradigm that lasted until his death in 1990.

The hardest time for my father in the fifty-seven years of our relationship had to be the year following the eighth grade at St. Gerard's when, somewhat on a whim, I went away to Kirkwood, Missouri, a suburb of St. Louis, to attend a Catholic seminary run by the Redemptorist priests who were the resident clergy at

St. Gerard's church and school. Dad, who never traveled out of the state of Texas until, at seventy, he came to New York to see his son the CEO, wasn't able to see or speak to me for an entire school year. He never said anything, but it must have pained him deeply when I was at the seminary. I saw my mother only once that year, at Christmas, when she and Dad scraped together enough cash to buy her a train ticket, and the family of one of the priests put her up in their home.

In those days, it was not all that unusual that an eighth grader in Catholic school would be persuaded to decide to study for the priesthood and leave his family to enroll in a seminary. We were somewhat unusual in that I was an only child. The reader will understand that a one-child Catholic family in that era was about as rare as somebody winning the lottery twice.

The way it happened was just what you'd imagine: A young priest representing the seminary visited our school and gave a glowing presentation about a boy's life at St. Joseph's. When he showed a film with scenes of the seminary's professionally organized baseball and soccer leagues and teenage boys playing in the snow, something seldom if ever seen in South Texas, I was hooked. To prove I wasn't simply gullible and without serious intent, I was appropriately impressed by the presentation's portrayal of the seminary's high academic standards. And the allure of the religious component, including the missionary life of the Redemptorist Order of priests in foreign lands, also helped to convince this thirteen-year-old, who was the president of the eighth grade and the first acolyte among St. Gerard's altar boys, that this was something I had to do. Two other members of my class of about fifty boys and girls made the same decision.

It was a truly great year and delivered on everything I had expected, especially the quality of the education and the sports program, where I proved I could hold my own with those northern kids, some of whom, we were told, ended up playing for the New York Yankees or St. Louis Cardinals. It's true I was terribly homesick for the first few weeks and asked to go back to San Antonio to be with my ailing mother, but those feelings passed, and when the end of the school year came around I really didn't want to go home for the summer.

Of course, I did have to go home, and after saying so long to all my new friends and vowing to resume our friendships in September, I boarded the Missouri Pacific and headed for San Antonio. It was during this train ride that I was coaxed by one of the older seminarians into lighting up the only cigarette I've ever smoked.

The summer was great, and reuniting with my parents had all the appeal I remembered from my younger days. And in mid-July on a terribly hot Texas night there was a significant event: The girl next door came over to have ice-cold watermelon with my family. Later that night I told my parents I didn't want to go back to the seminary. Think what you will; I was fourteen years old!

My father picked up my cultural education where he left off the summer before. In this mission, he was assisted by his twin brother, Arthur, who was, like him, an immensely talented writer, performer, graphic artist, public speaker, and producer/director of various types of entertainment. If the stock market crash of 1929 and the Great Depression hadn't devastated working families, I have no doubt my dad's career would have resembled mine more than the life he actually lived.

Arthur played a larger than typical role for an uncle in those years, in part because he had no children and I was the only child of his twin. He called me "Junior," the name other family members insisted on calling me, to my chagrin. Unhappily, the window of Uncle Art's influence was relatively short. He became an award-winning photographer for the *San Antonio Light*, the newspaper I would head years later, during the period of the swashbuckling newspaper world that was portrayed in Ben Hecht and Charlie MacArthur's 1920s Broadway play *The Front Page*. That environment, coupled with whatever gene that produces alcoholism in otherwise sane and virtuous humans, limited his lifetime achievements.

As my generation vividly recalls, the Great Depression caused massive unemployment and a litany of difficult life conditions. Among the many jobs my dad landed was driving a delivery truck for the Colgate-Palmolive-Peet Company, as that great American corporation was known then. I can still picture Dad standing alongside his brown Colgate panel truck.

Dad got "laid off" from Colgate—"laid off" being the term created, I think, in that horrible period, and still used today, to distinguish between losing your job for reasons related to your performance and getting fired nonetheless because your services were no longer needed in a shrinking economic environment.

Somebody told Dad that the Postal Service had developed a system that let unemployed and able-bodied men sit in what they called the "swing room" and occasionally catch a "shift" as a letter carrier. Additionally, your name could go on a list that might one day make a permanent postal job available, when and if there were vacancies. Those long days in the swing room were brutal for my dad, my mom, and me. He wasn't making enough money to keep the family together, so he sent my mother and me for much of a year to my grandfather Connally's farmhouse in Union Valley, about fifty miles from San Antonio. This was a small dirt farm with the obligatory privy, no electricity, and no running water. Dad came to visit as often as he could, hitchhiking most of the way but usually having to walk much of the way.

I remember Dad navigating the grueling trip at Easter, mostly on foot, in a driving rain with a baby bunny in hand. Both he and the bunny looked drowned as he approached the house in Union Valley, walking among the watermelons and peanuts that were the only crops the moisture-starved farm would sustain.

The resilient Frank Bennack weathered that difficult period, always in good humor, and on what a "temporary man" could earn from Uncle Sam's Postal Service, until he was finally able to bring Mom and me home. That day came in 1939, when Dad announced the glorious news that he would become a "regular man," a full-time, civil-service-protected letter carrier. He had worked hard, year after uncertain year, as if the work were its own reward, and then he was tangibly rewarded. The long nightmare of job uncertainty was over while the national savior, Franklin Delano Roosevelt, was only in his second term.

◆

When FDR died, I was out riding the first bike I ever got. The thirty-second president was so beloved in our household that when Mom heard of his death, she walked all over the neighborhood until she found me and forced me to come inside the house for fear something horrible was about to befall the United States of America.

After becoming a "regular man," Dad never considered giving up that civil service job. He saw himself as a dedicated public servant, and he made as much success out of it as can be made carrying a mail sack on one's back. Everyone on his route loved him. I don't think he ever had a dog bite him. The nuns at a convent on his route showered him with coffee and pastries, handmade sachets and knitted mufflers that were hardly needed in San Antonio's thermal climate. He served as president of the local chapter of the National Association of Letter Carriers, the postman's union of that day, and finally got the sack off his back after thirty years, when he was put in charge of a neighborhood post office not far from our rented house.

The Dad I knew best was not the worker who delivered mail. It was the eternal enthusiast who took advantage of the security and predictable hours of his job to fill his free time with acting, painting in oils, and producing shows. He gained a reputation as an umpire for a near-professional level of amateur baseball. He bought a loudspeaker system and managed political rallies for local politicians. He made extra money as the announcer at jalopy car races and read scripture aloud at our Catholic Church on Sunday morning.

And he took me along and often engaged me directly in every one of these activities.

He regularly put on a catcher's mitt and caught the curveballs he had taught me how to throw for hours in our driveway. He coached me, informally, in my American Legion–sponsored high school baseball league, well enough to help me qualify as one of only two members of my team to make the citywide all-star game, sponsored, amazingly it now seems, by Hearst.

CHAPTER 2

The Teenage Dick Clark

B efore I had my own dreams, I took my cues from my father. In my preteens, I followed him around as he pursued every local theater opportunity. When he was in a play, I learned everyone's lines. When he asked me to perform, there was no question about my participation, which is how I played a shoeshine boy reciting a tribute to my mother in the variety shows he produced. Later, I adapted jokes from *The Complete Book of Patter* or *The Pocket Book of Jokes* for the emcee assignments I got in my teens. So when I decided not to return to the seminary and reentered St. Gerard's high school in the tenth grade, I looked forward to team sports, but maybe even more I looked forward to whatever might come next for me in show business.

Elmer Kosub—"Flash Kosub," as he was called—was a rare high school faculty member who went on to become a genuine legend as baseball coach for St. Mary's University, where he won 501 games and 16 conference titles. Not only did he very successfully coach our winning high school football team (I was a 149-pound running back), he created and supervised a high school entertainment activity he named the Mighty Little Opera Company, an acting troupe that featured high school kids with sing-ing, acting, musical, and comedic talent. Teens from rival schools were welcome, but we really didn't need them—there was a lot of talent in the two hundred kids from our high school. The shows we put on were in the 1930s mold of the Mickey Rooney/Judy Garland movies: upbeat musical stories of kids with life or family challenges, which always prompted the response "Let's put on a show."

Kosub cast me in a variety of roles in the Mighties shows. More often than not I was the emcee or announcer. Then other school groups, and sometimes even adult organizations, recruited me to play that role for their shows. Bear in mind this was before the introduction of television in local communities. There was a great deal of live entertainment, especially in supper clubs; I was good enough to be hired by Sevenoaks, the most highly regarded San Antonio supper club of the time.

At one of those gigs, Bud Whaley, who combined the role of lead announcer with program scout for local radio station KMAC, approached me. Would I be interested in doing a Saturday morn-ing DJ show for teenagers? This junior in high school promptly said yes.

The station's professionals included a fellow named Harry O'Conner, known as "Mushmouth." Years later, we met again: He became the agent/manager for Governor Ronald Reagan's radio programs and newspaper columns in the years leading up to the presidential run.

Show business banter is one of the perks of the trade. Between shows, one of the DJs quipped that they were teaching me how to operate a control room and the next thing they knew they would hear that I was in Los Angeles, making $60 a week. Sixty dollars! That would translate to about $650 in today's dollars, well below what you'd think would be a good salary at a Los Angeles radio station; back then, it struck me as a princely wage. But I recall one of the DJs complaining about both the level of his pay and the untimely paychecks, saying the station manager was "the only guy I ever met who could live without money."

I was promised some modest compensation, but I don't recall if I ever received it. It didn't matter. KMAC was hardly the most prestigious or successful San Antonio radio station, but there were enough listeners to make a kid feel like a local celebrity. And the experience was great: I was allowed the privilege of a small studio audience and total control over the records I spun. My theme song was Glenn Miller's "A String of Pearls," and Ella Fitzgerald was my favorite artist; I introduced her in my practiced radio baritone as "the world's greatest singer." All these years later, friends still tell me they hear a radio voice when I speak in public.

The experience at KMAC was more valuable than I knew at the time. It taught me, among other lessons, that as long as I conducted myself respectfully, I didn't have to be intimidated by the rich and famous. As a teenager running around with a wire recorder—the forerunner of tape recorders and video recorders—I was able to talk my way backstage to secure interviews with some big names of the day during their San Antonio road shows. These included international movie beauty Yvonne De Carlo; band leader Xavier Cugat, a leading figure in the spread of Latin music; his gorgeous then-not-much-older-than-me spouse, Abbe Lane; and among others, Russ Morgan, the composer-orchestra leader who had four songs on the charts in 1949, "So Tired" and "Cruising Down the River" capturing the number three and number one spots, respectively.

KMAC, 630 kHz, limped on until the early 1980s and is best remembered for the KMAC Green Neon Clocks that the station distributed for promotional purposes in the 1950s. Those clocks are now valuable collector's items.

◆

The first licensed television station in San Antonio was WOAI-TV, which launched on December 11, 1949. To introduce this amazing new technology to a small but anxiously anticipatory group of TV set owners, the station televised an extravaganza of sorts, featuring "talented students" from the city's high schools and colleges. I did my stand-up comedy routine in the cavernous Joe Freeman Coliseum and was rewarded with my picture in the *San Antonio Express-News* alongside Anna Nell Walters, a pal who danced for that first-ever television audience as she did for my show numerous times later.

The second station to be licensed to San Antonio was KEYL, channel 5. It went on the air on February 15, 1950. Neither station had much programming, so both conducted auditions for people who hosted radio programs, and, even better, those with loyal radio audiences. Somehow, I made the grade with KEYL, and at the tender age of seventeen I became the writer, talent booker, sponsorship salesman, and emcee of my own thirty-minute television show on Sunday nights. We planned to call the show *Teen Canteen*, and set it as if there were a group of teenagers gathered around a drugstore soda fountain. The station's lawyer discovered somebody already had registered the name, so in a quick pivot we came up with *Time for Teens*, set in that staple of network talk shows: a couch, a host's desk, and a musical performance stage.

Because I have for years referred to myself as the "poor man's Dick Clark," people who have heard about my stint on *Time for Teens* think of it as a dance show. But the rock music that propelled the real Dick Clark show to fame in the 1950s was just being born; my show was a display of performances by young people, singers, dancers, and accordion players. Our highlight was a weekly competition for a teen queen. Helping to choose a girl who got a bunch of swag for being named the Teen Queen of the Week— that was really good work for a teenage boy.

Time for Teens lasted a couple of years and generated a fair following for its time. There was no videotape then, so there are no recordings of the show I can use to torture the grandkids. I've tracked down some newspaper stories and pictures that evoke fond memories: The best one has the station's program director, Bill Robb, and me standing by an impressive stack of mail. I'm quite sure most of it was favorable.

Many years later, when I met the real Dick Clark in connection with his role as producer of a show at The Museum of Television & Radio (today known as The Paley Center for Media), I told him about my unauthorized use of his name. He loved the comparison, and graciously said, "Looking at our respective career paths, I disagree about 'the poor man's Dick Clark.'"

With my dad's help, I persuaded Robb and his wife, Harriet, who served as an assistant program director, to green-light an audience-participation show called *Who's Your Friend?* One of the sponsors was an auto dealer. The studio was on the mezzanine level of what was then the tallest building in San Antonio. Remember, no videotape. I had to get the car into the studio. That meant putting down tracks like you see on the trucks that transport cars and driving the car up to the mezzanine level. And then, after the show, driving it back down with Luella Mae Smith—my girlfriend, who later became my wife—watching with trepidation.

I don't ever remember being nervous. I had enough confidence that I always felt I could pull it off, even though I usually worked without a script. I thought I ad-libbed maybe better than I really did. During one of the shows I apparently described pretty much everything as being "wonderful"—after the show, Bill Robb said fewer "wonderfuls" would be appreciated. I took it as a learning lesson; I wasn't offended.

These early experiences on the stage, as a radio DJ and as a television host, contributed in a major way to whatever success I had as a media executive. So much of what a company like Hearst does depends on developing audiences; knowing what audiences will favorably respond to is a key executive skill. But in those heady teen years I wasn't thinking how I could translate what I was learning into a practical career—there's no one as confident as a kid who's had a taste of show business success.

CHAPTER 3

You Can't Make Your Way Alone.
Find a Mentor.

When it came to learning about hands-on experience and grounding in life, Frank A. Bennack Sr. was for me in a class by himself. Later, there were other mentors. I've learned over my long life that among the most successful strategies for success is finding and following mentors who can not only teach you but help push you up the ladder.

The late William Randolph Hearst Jr., the second son and namesake of our company's founder, always got a knowing smile when he said he got ahead in life because of "help from an older guy." For Bill, that older guy was William Randolph Hearst. Bill's humorous recognition of the role of mentors, superiors, and elders in one's life certainly resonated with me, because I may have gotten a bigger boost from the older generation than almost anybody I know.

Some of my first mentors were the School Sisters of Notre Dame, who taught both the elementary and high schools at St. Gerard's. Sister Mary Louise was about four-foot-ten. She dressed in the severe nun's habit of the day, always resembling a penguin in full trot. She was convinced that I could bring our debating and oratorical team to victory in competitions despite our meager school population, and she spent many hours helping me hone my command of the necessary skills. I think those skills have been as much the key to my rising up the corporate ladder, maybe more, than any other ability I've developed. Learning early how to speak with conviction apparently led others to grasp what I was saying and to believe I was honest and trustworthy, which I always strived to be, and not motivated only by a calculated hope of personal gain. An invaluable lesson.

Thanks to Sister Mary Louise and our ROTC instructor, Captain Evans, I was appointed cadet colonel and commanding officer of our Junior ROTC unit despite finishing second in the school-wide "Simon Says" military drilling competition. I began to think that second place wasn't so bad; after all, there is third place and fourth place and even one-hundredth place in some endeavors. Still, second place wasn't what my mentors wanted for me, and more importantly, what they expected from me.

My luck turned when, after being judged second in a citywide oratorical contest sponsored, again amazingly by Hearst, the primary sponsor—Colonel B. J. Horner, publisher of Hearst's *San Antonio Light* newspaper—decided the judges he had appointed were wrong. He privately declared me the winner, saying that anyone who "could talk like that" could certainly sell advertising. He then gave me the real prize: a job offer as a classified ad salesman for his newspaper. I had turned seventeen years old in February, and the job was to start as soon as I graduated from high school in May. I had earned a two-year scholarship to St. Mary's University in one of the high school oratorical contests, but the discussion about what I should do lasted only a few minutes in the Bennack household. As soon as you're old enough to work . . . get a job. Higher education could wait. I accepted Colonel Horner's offer.

B. J. Horner had been a captain in World War I and rose to the rank of full colonel in the Second World War, serving with great distinction as G2, senior intelligence officer, on the staff of military icon George S. Patton. His career path at the newspaper had seen him rise to the position of advertising director before World War II, and, shortly after his return from the war, publisher, the newspaper's top job. Like Patton, he was tough as nails. When a raccoon crawled through an open window in his living room, he pulled out his 12-gauge shotgun and blasted away, splattering the raccoon's blood all over the walls, furniture, and carpets. You never know whether stories like this are at least in part apocryphal, but it was said that the blast was loud enough for a neighbor lady to call the police, believing the old colonel must have gone off his rocker.

◆

Now that I had a full-time job selling classified advertising for the *San Antonio Light* and a serious girlfriend still in school who I wanted to marry someday, it seemed unlikely that I'd be inspired to move to a larger TV market to secure a future career path in that field. I valued and greatly enjoyed my TV shows and was allowed to continue to do them after going to work for the newspaper. I took the television work seriously and tried to do my best at it without any infringement on my newspaper job. I signed up for voice lessons so I could present myself as a singing emcee in the style of Arthur Godfrey, Bert Parks, and other TV hosts of the period. My mother said she couldn't watch when I did that! My uncle

Arthur, a talented thespian, commented that I was modeling my singing after the popular crooners of the day, something he didn't think I could master. "You just aren't depraved enough to pull it off" was his assessment.

Did I have enough wit and charm to become a rival to Johnny Carson? Decades later, these questions would consume my daughters after a few exposures to my public appearances as a media executive who made pro bono appearances for good causes. This wasn't just kids asking their father some inevitable "What if?" questions. They had heard me quip from the stage of the Grand Ballroom at the Waldorf Astoria that "I have taken the microphone here enough nights to qualify for the Waldorf pension plan." My daughters concluded: Dad was good at this stuff.

Although I didn't realize it at the time, selling classified advertising turned out to be an extraordinary training ground for the roles I would later fill. Classifieds were then a critical part of the economic equation for newspapers, something I needed to understand as a local publisher and as the future head of the Hearst newspapers. In most American cities with more than one newspaper, the paper with the greatest classified volume was almost always the market leader. At some newspapers, classifieds represented the largest single source of revenue.

The classified section typically contained ads from businesses such as auto dealers, real estate agents, and employment agencies. Selling and constructing ad campaigns that worked for those businesses was an essential skill for success. Classifieds were also an important attraction for newspaper subscribers. They were the precursors of social media—citizens used the classified section for personal messages, to rent out their extra rooms, and to sell their unneeded sewing machine or bike. And then there was the sheer pleasure of reading classifieds. They told stories. They gave you the pulse of their communities. Classifieds were the modern version of the town bazaar.

Because my guaranteed newspaper pay was very small—$30 a week—and I got a penny commission for every line of classifieds I sold, the experience served as a first test of my ability to deliver in the business world by earning enough commission to live on. It also formed the basis for comparing my performance with the classified sellers working alongside me at the *Light* and at the competitive newspaper.

Selling classifieds was in no way glamorous. The classified ad seller was near the bottom rung at the paper. You started there, and you hoped to move up as quickly as possible.

◆

The period from the day Colonel Horner proclaimed me the winner of the oratorical contest to the day seventeen years later when I succeeded him as publisher of the *Light* was anything but straightforward. Along the way I left the company twice in order to make enough money to support a growing family; in between, I spent almost two years in the Army, from 1954 to 1956, most of that time at Robinson Barracks in Stuttgart, Germany. Given my media experience, I somewhat expected to be assigned to a special services unit, the GIs who arrange entertainment for the troops. Instead, prior to shipping me overseas the Army sent me to Fort Benjamin Harrison, northwest of Indianapolis, Indiana, to be trained as an Army postal clerk. Every Army post office required one such specially trained soldier. Not only did these post offices deliver mail to the troops, an essential task was the sale of postal money orders, the method many GIs used to send money home. We handled many millions of dollars performing that latter function. That was another kick for my dad. He had been a postman for most of his working life, and now his son was assigned to do postal work.

By virtue of its excellent college program in Europe, conducted by the University of Maryland, and the GI Bill that funded college tuition for veterans, the Army made it possible for me to get enough college education for both Maryland and St. Mary's University to count me as an alumnus. After returning to San Antonio from the Army, my life got too complicated—or so I argued at the time—for me to stay in night school at St. Mary's long enough to earn a degree. I took correspondence courses the Army offered, and studied economics and, briefly, even law by correspondence from LaSalle Extension University. Such courses were the by-mail predecessor to today's online studying.

I always have thought of myself as college educated, but it bothers me even today to have to qualify the nature of that college education. Much later in life I greatly enjoyed receiving an honorary doctorate from the University of the Incarnate Word in San Antonio; that and giving the commencement address in 2010 at the College of Communication at the University of Texas at Austin were the only times I donned the cap and gown after high school. Not unlike a lot of parents in my situation, I imagine, my own experience motivated me to help make it possible for my five daughters to collect nine college and graduate degrees.

The first time I left the *San Antonio Light* was to accept an offer to become a nineteen-year-old classified advertising manager for the legendary Pulitzer Prize–winning crusading editor and owner of the Greenville, Mississippi *Delta Democrat-Times*, Hodding Carter II. The second career detour away from Hearst and the newspaper business occurred a few years after I was discharged from the Army and returned to the *Light*. I was recruited to take a management role in a large retailer, Jorrie Furniture Company, that happened to be a major advertiser in our newspaper. As before, the motivation was a need for a greater income. There were now two baby girls in the Bennack household, and Luella had become a stay-at-home mom. (My decision was one of only two times in my entire career when I directly asked for a raise, and the only time I didn't get a "yes," giving me a 50-50 track record in that exercise.) Horner told me that because it was a decision about money I just might have my priorities wrong, but he said that he wouldn't stand in my way.

Getting the experience at the retailer was a boost to my standing even with Horner and Hearst. For the next couple of years I learned what it was like to be on the other side of the advertising equation. As the planner and buyer of advertising, I developed the media mix between newspapers, radio, television, and outdoor advertising, a very different experience from selling newspaper ads. Horner and his key deputies never lost track of me and always acted as if I were on loan and destined to return to the *Light* and Hearst.

In 1961 fate intervened again. The advertising director for the San Antonio paper, who was already thinking of stepping aside, fell and injured himself. Horner called. When we met, he described what he felt was a critical vulnerability for the newspaper that had to be dealt with immediately. He said that he had talked to G. O. Markuson, executive vice president of the Hearst Corporation and general manager of Hearst Newspapers, and "Mark" had authorized him to tell me to "name my price." Really? Yes. Anything reasonable would be acceptable to Hearst. It was 1961, and I named my price: $250 a week, a thousand dollars a year more than I was earning at the retailer. I probably left something on the table then, but it didn't matter. I returned to Hearst, where I spent the next fifty-six years, and counting.

In 1964, Horner appointed me assistant publisher and charged me with overseeing the newspaper's promotional activities along with some advertising, labor relations, and newsroom responsibilities. I quickly unwrapped my early radio and television experience and became the spokesman in the newspaper's TV ads, just as many CEOs would later do during an era of CEO-personalized corporate commercials.

Attracting young audiences to newspapers was, even then, a difficult task, so I bought into the newspaper's sponsorship and promotion of a Teen Fair to be held in the city's largest venue, the Joe Freeman Coliseum, starting on June 6, 1964. The Fair booked many of the great teen idols of the day: Lesley Gore, Bobby Vee, Bobby Rydell, and George Jones. They also booked a group I had never heard of. My daughter didn't roll her eyes at my ignorance; to Shelley and a couple of her girlfriends, I was the guy who made it possible for them to have their pictures taken with a fellow named Mick Jagger. In 1975, when the Rolling Stones returned to San Antonio, the *Express-News* reported that a "mixed crowd of cowboys and kids" had booed their 1964 performance at our Teen Fair. And the article noted that before going onstage in 1964 Jagger made a point to display his fire-engine-red bikini underwear—happily not in the presence of my ten-year-old daughter and her friends.

Central to that period was what I learned about the importance of the absence of office politics in corporate life. Later in my career I would see companies that were held back from success more by unbridled office politics than by the actions of their strongest competitors. My experience at our paper in San Antonio, in contrast, was a textbook case of dealing with change the right way. Although I was assuming the responsibilities and authority of the ad director, Tom Gish, I never saw any sign of hurt or resentment from him. To the contrary, he showed up at my home numerous Sunday mornings after church with buñuelos, a Mexican fried dough confection that the Bennack girls loved. My sense is that CEOs of too many companies fail to move swiftly to eradicate toxic office politics. To this day I weigh in quickly and heavily at any sign of it. This kind of distraction can drain all the energy out of otherwise competent management.

Not long after making me assistant publisher—this title, because of the time in my life it came, I may actually have valued more than any ever bestowed on me—Horner started to lay plans for me to succeed him as publisher. But once he made it known he would likely want to step down at some early date, he got more help from New York than he wanted; management asked him to hire a well-known executive who was out of a job because of the recent shutdown of another Hearst newspaper and groom him as a successor. Horner quickly decided he might have to stay a year or two longer at the *Light* in order to convince New York that this Bennack "kid" was ready to take over.

Horner stayed in the publisher's chair until, at seventy-two, he was authorized to turn the *Light* over to me, which he did on December 6, 1967, when I was the ripe old age of thirty-four.

◆

Characteristically, Horner performed one more indispensable service for me that may well have allowed me, years later, to be ready for greater responsibilities. In June of 1968, about seven months after I became publisher of the *Light*, the senior leadership of Hearst decided to hold a quarterly board meeting in San Antonio during HemisFair, the first and only world's fair in San Antonio history, held on the occasion of the city's 250th anniversary. It was a great time for San Antonio and for me, because Horner looked to me to be the paper's representative to the endless planning activities leading up to the fair—it was an opportunity for me to build relationships with local leaders like auto dealer/investor B.J. "Red" McCombs, premier banker Tom C. Frost, energy activist/ banker William Sinkin, former Navy WAVE turned city council member/mayor Lila Cockrell, and construction company giant H.B. Zachry. They were changing San Antonio and I was welcome to their "club."

But a shadow hung over that 180-day event. The assassination of Martin Luther King occurred on April 4, two days before the opening of the fair, and the killing of Robert Kennedy on June 5 made it difficult to feel the bright future that a world's fair promises. But there was no thought of postponing the long-scheduled meeting of the Hearst Board.

Among other events for that June get-together, we planned a dinner at the Tower of the Americas, the signature structure that still rivals the Alamo as a recognizable symbol of the city. The evening went off beautifully, although it became clear that I was a rookie on the subject of wine. To these heavy-hitter Hearst executives, mostly from New York and Los Angeles, I served Lancers, a medium sweet, lightly sparkling wine popular with the $6-a-bottle crowd. In his after-dinner remarks, William Randolph Hearst Jr. looked at me and said, "As to the wine, kid, it's Lavoris—but a good year." My education as a corporate host had begun.

HemisFair also gave me my first close-up experience with a senior Hearst family member: W. R. Hearst Jr. I knew that Bill often praised the military in his weekly column and that there was a large military population stationed at multiple Air Force and Army bases near San Antonio. The idea was obvious: persuade Bill to give a speech at HemisFair's main auditorium during the board's stay.

Bill, not surprisingly, wowed a packed house of civic and military leaders with a patriotic and provocative speech. But it wasn't until I met him in his suite at the St. Anthony Hotel that I got a full-bodied introduction to the personality of the founder's namesake and best-known son. Bill had just stepped out of the shower. Wrapped only in a towel, he was talking on the phone to his wife, Austine. The subject appeared to be the Bolshoi Ballet, which was appearing in San Antonio during that week. Ballet. Nearly naked man. Bill Hearst was, clearly, an interesting character.

It soon became clear that Bill had a brilliant and sometimes biting wit. I remember his comment that night about a public official: "He has all the characteristics of a dog, except loyalty." He then transitioned to a serious discussion about the Company, its present status, and his views of the future. He solicited mine. I shared some thoughts.

Then he looked me straight in the eye and said something like this: "You're building quite a reputation for such a young executive. What is your ultimate personal goal in the company?"

"I would hope one day to qualify myself to be the president and chief executive of Hearst," I said boldly, with less than ideal diplomacy.

"That's a tall order," he responded. "Good for you!"

When I became CEO, ten years later, Bill reminded me of that night in San Antonio and remarked that if I could deliver on every goal with equal success I'd be a very effective president.

◆

A few days after the New York contingent returned home, I got a warm note from G. O. Markuson, the general manager of Hearst Newspapers, thanking me for a job well done and telling me that he would be out of service for a few days while he underwent surgery. Stunningly, Mark died in the hospital, a virtually unheard-of outcome after prostate surgery even in those days.

The last time I had been in New York was to formalize my promotion to publisher. During that meeting Mark was so pleased to hand such a key job to a thirty-four-year-old—and to increase my compensation to a robust $30,000 a year—that he literally had tears rolling down his cheeks. Now, shocked and saddened, Horner and I traveled to New York to bury Mark.

Horner and I made it through the terrible days as we witnessed the turmoil that accompanied the sudden loss of the second most senior Hearst corporate officer and the most senior newspaper official. A few days after we returned home, Horner asked me to have lunch with him at La Louisiane, our favorite and arguably the city's most prestigious restaurant. There he revealed that while we were in New York there had been some discussion among the board members about possibly bringing me to New York. Frank Massi, the company's CFO, had been chosen to assume Markuson's position as executive vice president, effectively COO, and the message was that there was some support for my taking over the newspaper general manager role, despite my having been publisher in San Antonio less than a year. "I told them absolutely not," Horner said. "This newspaper which I have spent my life building needs you, and furthermore you are nowhere near ready for that job!"

Sadly, Colonel B. J. Horner died shortly after our trip to bury Markuson and only ten months after he had retired, struck down by the massive stroke he had long feared. With his death, I lost a mentor and supporter almost as essential as my father.

I never knew how serious that consideration of me for that job actually was, but shortly after Horner's death, Joseph Kingsbury-Smith, the onetime publisher of the *New York Journal-American* and at that time Hearst Newspaper European director and chief foreign writer, and importantly a director of the Company and a trustee of the Hearst Family Trust, sent me a letter:

> It was with profound sorrow that I read your cable
> advising me of the passing of BJ. I found it this morning
> on my return to Rome from Sardinia. I know how deeply
> distressed you must be by the loss of that grand gentleman
> who thought so highly of you. . . . BJ's death at this time is
> doubly disappointing to me because, confidentially, I fear
> it will mean that management will be reluctant to take
> you away from the Light. I was hoping that with the tragic

loss of Mark, we might be able to bring you to New York to become general manager of the newspapers. Now I am afraid there would be a reluctance to risk taking you away from San Antonio. I am, however, confident that the day will come when, if you wish it, the New York job will be yours.

I still have that letter, dated September 11, 1968.

One piece of good fortune followed the sadness: the transfer of supervising me from Horner's personal mentorship to the New York brass. That partly had to do with Horner's making known his belief about the role I might ultimately play in the company after a reasonable apprenticeship as a local publisher and telling the New York brass not to let me get away from the Company again. Talk about the value of mentors.

◆

In 1970, after I'd been at the helm of the *San Antonio Light* for two years, we completed a major expansion of the paper's production facilities. It was truly a big deal for any local newspaper: a multi-million-dollar pressroom that would not only allow later deadlines because of the "amazing speed" of the new equipment, but would enable color printing, which up until then was virtually unknown at local newspapers.

I thought this was a unique opportunity to show off this important Hearst investment to advertisers, local, state, and federal officials, and other VIPs who were about to be introduced to newspaper printing quality not previously seen. So we decided to have a luncheon in the pressroom with a white tablecloth gourmet meal, after which we would have a dedication ceremony—an audacious idea, considering the usual spread of printer's ink from shoes to hands and even to clothes in a pressroom. Further, as our guests departed, we planned to give them just-printed full-color copies of that day's newspaper containing not only the latest news but also pictures of the guests themselves, taken as they arrived for our lunch and press launch. We invited about two hundred guests from our local list and several key Hearst executives.

Showing up from the home office were Richard Berlin, the company's CEO, who had succeeded W. R. Hearst after his death and who was the only successor CEO who had actually known the founder; George Hearst, eldest son of the founder; Frank Massi, executive vice president and COO of the company; and John Sacchia, Hearst's vice president of production, who had helped me sell the press project to general management. I proudly stood at the entryway to the pressroom and introduced Messrs. Berlin, Massi, and George Hearst to every guest. Because these men and women made up so much of my business life, I was able to introduce all two hundred of them without notes. I frankly didn't think much about it. These were people with whom I lived and in many cases was in almost daily contact.

I later learned that Berlin was hugely impressed that the Texas "kid" was able to introduce every person who came through the door without a note or a prompter, and that he often talked to his New York associates about that "feat" as if I had done something extraordinary. I'm told he began to lay the groundwork for me to be brought into New York management. When I made trips to New York after that, Berlin would have me stop by for a chat. The best part of those meetings was something he'd do as I was leaving his office: He'd make a hand signal intended for his influential executive assistant, rubbing his right thumb across the fingers on that hand. I later learned that meant for the assistant to see to it that "we pay this kid some more money."

That obviously didn't happen after every meeting with Berlin, but later I learned to look for it, and, several times, I soon received a raise. That experience probably was most responsible for my never again asking for raises and relying on those decisions to be made willingly by my superiors. Most advisers would conclude that's a losing strategy, but it worked for me. For those looking for life lessons and career advice, here's an example, one of many I've encountered, where conventional wisdom didn't apply.

◆

Despite the talk in New York, the idea of moving to the Hearst home office wasn't by any means top of mind in 1968. For me, there was no more gratifying job than publisher of my home-town's leading daily newspaper. And those years in San Antonio were just as gratifying from a family perspective.

A couple with five children at every level of education, from kindergarten to high school, at the same time, and one parent, the father, working sixty hours a week—that is a description of a heroic wife and mother. It was no secret then, or now, that Luella played the major role in supporting our girls and managing their lives. She served as president of more than one parent and teacher association, and brought her very willing husband to many paren-tal events at the kids' schools. The only downside of those eve-nings was those minuscule school desks. After our girls grew past grade school, I vowed never again to squeeze into one of those classroom desks—a vow I couldn't keep once grandchildren came along. In addition to her parenting and school commitments, she joined me in hosting HemisFair. She was acknowledged by having a barge on the San Antonio River named "The Luella" during my year as Chamber of Commerce president. "The Luella" served as an unusual but ideal venue for entertaining VIPs, as well as Bennack family excursions.

That didn't seem enough recognition for all Luella did for our family, so on her thirty-fifth birthday I bought her a mile-long, 1970 Cadillac Brougham that cost a then incredible $8,000. When we moved to New Canaan, Connecticut, we were so embarrassed to be driving that gas-guzzling, tugboat-size vehicle that we quickly downsized Luella to a Jeep.

1969 to 1975 were vintage years. We attended every football game during our oldest daughter Shelley's 1971 high school senior year at Robert E. Lee, including the team's victory in the state championship game in the Dallas Cowboys' new stadium. Shelley went on from there to get a law degree at the University of Virginia, and among other achievements helped form an all-woman law firm. Laura, our second oldest, who now has accounting, law, and medical degrees, proudly marched with the Robert E. Lee Rebel Rousers, as the school's performing pep squad was called in those days. (After years of controversy, in 2017 the school board voted to change the school's name simply to "Lee.") And we looked on with excitement as four of our five daughters, Shelley, Laura, Diane, and Cindi, were filmed along the San Antonio River as "extras"—and hobnobbed with movie stars John Astin and Peter Ustinov—in the 1969 movie *Viva Max!* The show business bug bit Diane, Cindi, and Julie, our youngest, and all three gave it a fling.

And one quiet thrill. As anyone who has been able to do it knows, it was deeply satisfying for us to buy Luella's and my parents—Luella's dad was a career Army master sergeant and my dad a letter carrier—better houses in neighborhoods they never imagined they could live in, making us feel like loving children who were truly respectful of all they had done for us.

Not every experience was so upbeat. In January 1969, and for weeks thereafter, a public menace who called himself "The Thief of Baghdad" literally terrorized San Antonio with a series of residential break-ins. They generally occurred while residents were at home; the victims reported not only robberies but also violence. While the intruder remained at large there were few, if any, light moments in the city's frightened households, but an incident that occurred in the Bennack household remains one of the family's most often repeated tales all these years later.

Things had gotten tense enough that for the first time ever I kept a loaded shotgun under our bed. In the middle of this particular night Luella and I were awakened by a loud crash that sounded as if it had come from the area of our front door, a door partially made of glass. I bolted out of bed and rushed to the front hall, shotgun in hand. One by one, almost instantly it seemed, all five Bennack girls gathered to peer over the railing that ran the full length of the hall connecting their upstairs bedrooms. I quickly discovered that the chandelier that had graced our entry foyer had broken loose from its hook and chain and landed with an enormous thud. No "Thief of Baghdad" in sight.

"Daddy shot the chandelier," one of our daughters pronounced in her loudest voice.

All returned to normal when Samuel Webb was arrested on

May 2, 1969, charged with the "Thief of Baghdad" crimes, and sentenced to ninety-nine years in prison.

◆

Tragedy struck on August 2, 1970. Mom, who had enjoyed the best health of her life for the last five years, passed away suddenly from what seemed like more of an accident than an illness. She had developed phlebitis in her leg, apparently caused by an injury that formed a clot, so her doctor put her in the hospital for observation. The next morning, Dad called her to say he was on his way to see her. During their conversation, the clot broke loose and triggered a fatal heart attack. Mom was just sixty-two. We were all stunned.

Luella and I and our two older girls got the news in Murray Bay, Quebec. As guests of Dick Berlin, Hearst's CEO, we might as well have been on another planet—in the very different world that existed then, Berlin spent the entire month of August at his Canadian home. Getting back from this remote location wasn't our only challenge. Luella and I had an ironclad rule of never flying together until Shelley, then sixteen, was at least eighteen. Luella and Laura took the only available commercial flights. Shelley and I flew back to the States on a small private prop plane Berlin arranged for us.

I was mourning. Dad was beyond sad. Really, he was broken; he simply could not be consoled. He had been happily retired, spending satisfying hours making oil and acrylic paintings of Texas landscapes that family and friends enthusiastically hung in their homes. All of that stopped cold.

And then he recovered. Less than a year after Mom died, Dad

told me he was going to marry Velma Hubbarth, an absolutely delightful sixty-year-old widow who worked at the supermarket where he and Mom shopped. And at age sixty-three, Frank Bennack Sr. experienced an emotional rebirth by virtue of a surprise relationship that led to a twenty-year marriage. He was the old Frank Bennack, closely monitoring my life and progress—because Dad never really believed I could be fully in charge, he often asked, "Is Mr. Hearst still happy with the job you're doing, son?"—and the lives of our children. He energetically resumed his writing and his landscape paintings.

Dad was in reasonably good health until 1988, when emphysema struck, the product of a lifetime habit of three packs of Camels or Lucky Strikes a day. On several occasions during the last few years of his life, he was so sick that his doctors urged me to rush home from New York. I must have made that trip five or six times, each time believing it would be the last. Then the false alarms ended, and Dad died, at eighty-two.

The lack of surprise didn't make Dad's death easier for me, and I struggled as I did his eulogy in my boyhood church in front of his thespian and postal friends, my friends, co-workers from the *San Antonio Light*, and many of the newspaper's clients. The tribute overflowed the church.

Velma had helped Dad to recover from Mom's death, and she knew the best way to help herself recover from Dad's—to step briskly into her new life. She did that admirably. She lived in the same retirement home for another nineteen years to an age just months short of one hundred, and was almost never without a gentleman friend.

CHAPTER 4

Hail to Local Publishers, Editors, Broadcasters, and Journalists

E very thinking citizen suddenly realized the risks of covering local news when five employees of the *Capital Gazette* newspaper in Anne Arundel County, Maryland, were murdered on June 28, 2018.

Although I doubt they gave it much thought until recently, it is likely our fellow citizens knew that journalists can and do from time to time work in harm's way. To be sure, most Americans paid close attention to the brutal details of the murder in the Saudi consulate in Istanbul, Turkey, of *Washington Post* columnist Jamal Khashoggi.

There is also—although maybe more in years past than today— a general recognition that news media is influential in our society. In February 1968, at the end of his newscast, Walter Cronkite declared the Vietnam War a "stalemate," a polite way of saying "unwinnable." Lyndon Johnson's comment to his aide, George Christian—"If I've lost Cronkite, I've lost Middle America"— spoke volumes. But the recognition of media importance too often solely relates to national news organizations, or at least news organizations that have national influence.

As a participant and firsthand observer I acknowledge the importance of the national media and its impact on the nation's life. I'm also aware of the far-reaching influence and impact these organizations, and especially their founders, have had outside the strict business of covering the news or delivering entertainment to our living rooms.

Leonard Goldenson, founder of what is now ABC, a valuable partner of Hearst, and my dear friend, and his wife, Isabelle, were cofounders of United Cerebral Palsy, today the fifth largest health charity in the United States. DeWitt Wallace, cofounder of *Reader's Digest* and his wife, Lila Bell, were prodigious philanthropists, donating their massive fortune to Macalester College, Colonial Williamsburg, and a wide array of arts and charitable organizations. The Wallaces ensured that after their deaths the foundation they created and funded would continue to support charitable causes, notably education and youth activities.

William S. Paley, the CEO who built CBS from a small radio organization into one of the nation's foremost television and radio powerhouses, chaired and endowed the Museum of Modern Art, supported the Newhouse School at Syracuse and the library at Temple, and founded and endowed the Museum of Broadcasting—later The Museum of Television & Radio and today known as The Paley Center for Media, an institution that arguably is our most valuable archive of the history of radio and television. The name changes of this valuable institution over its half-century history have followed the real-life changes in media. "Broadcasting" seemed inadequate after cable networks changed the game, and "Television & Radio" seemed inadequate in a world of Internet adoption. Thus: The Paley Center. I take special pride in the work "the Paley" has done. Largely because of my long service, Paley Center made me the recipient of the first Paley Honors. Then the Center got serious and broadened this prestigious award by giving it to women in television and those in the African American, Latino, and LGBTQ communities who have made an indelible mark on television and whose civil rights and roles in today's society have been advanced by the commitment of television networks and local stations. By telling their stories and engaging their talents in the drama, comedy, news, and sports programming that television brings into our homes, the industry and Paley have made those of us engaged singularly proud.

The Paley Center's additional role is to act as a convener of today's leaders in and out of media to further understanding of an evolving media landscape and to stimulate debate about its role. Disclosure: I am the only chairman of the Paley Center other than Mr. Paley himself. In the thirty years I've served in that capacity I have been privileged to work with three truly gifted presidents of this fine institution, Robert Batscha, Pat Mitchell, and today's staff leader, Maureen Reidy.

I'm compelled to add that, along with the role of the Hearst Corporation as a national and international media organization, William Randolph Hearst and his philanthropic mother endowed many educational, artistic, and charitable causes, among them two foundations that are active today in making grants in virtually every state, regardless of the presence or absence of Hearst business units.

My point: The national media organizations and their founders not only fostered organizations that deserved their designation as the Fourth Estate but also did good while doing well.

◆

It is often said that all politics is local. More than politics is local. Because political reality depends on what happens in cities and local communities, a number of local media giants have literally been the key to the growth and the quality of life in the cities their media properties serve.

Since I am a Texan by birth, I give you the story of a Texas media giant as the first example of this thesis.

Amon Giles Carter, who was born in the small town of Crafton, Texas, in 1879 and lived in Fort Worth from 1906 to 1955, made a statement that supports this thesis about as well as anybody could: "A man cannot live off his community; he must live with it." And he said: "You can't keep taking presents off the tree unless you put some on." Boy, did he mean it!

Carter first worked as a $35-a-week ad manager for the *Fort Worth Star*, the weaker rival of the *Fort Worth Telegram*. Within two years he convinced an investor to buy the more powerful and successful *Telegram* and make him the business manager of the combined papers. (It's interesting that our oldest media form, newspapers, were already combining to stay alive and healthy in 1908.) From 1923 until World War II, the *Star-Telegram* had the largest circulation of any newspaper in the South. Carter followed up by creating WBAP, the oldest radio station in Fort Worth, and followed that with Texas's first television station, WBAP-TV, in 1948.

His commercial success was impressive. I'm more impressed that he became the spokesman for Fort Worth and West Texas, effectively becoming the city's and the region's leading citizen. Along the way, using a Texas cowboy image and friendships cultivated with the likes of Will Rogers and Hearst's own Walter Winchell, Carter promoted business and government spending for his home region. He is credited to have been largely responsible for a four-year college for Lubbock authorized by the Texas legislature, now called Texas Tech, where he served as first chairman of the board. He's said to have played a key role in getting the predecessor company of American Airlines to move its headquarters to adjacent Dallas, although he had a well-known competition with, and antipathy toward, the larger Dallas. He influenced Airforce Plant 4, now Lockheed Martin Aeronautics, and Bell Aircraft, now Bell Helicopter Textron, to come to Fort Worth. Enough educational, community and artistic centers bear, or once bore, his name to have satisfied a dozen movers and shakers. The Amon Carter Museum of American Art was established sixty years ago in part to house his collection of paintings and sculpture by Frederic Remington (who, incidentally, worked for Hearst during the Spanish-American War) and Charles Russell. It remains an extraordinarily valuable regional cultural asset and magnet for tourists, students, and art lovers alike. It would be hard to think of a more significant influence on a great American city and region than that of Amon Giles Carter on Fort Worth, Texas.

◆

I came to know of another newspaper owner named Carter, who faced more immediate personal challenges. As I mentioned earlier, in the 1950s I worked for William Hodding Carter II, the principal owner and editor of the *Delta Democrat-Times*, in Greenville, Mississippi. He was also an author who stood far outside the Mississippi political norms of his time.

He was born in Hammond, Louisiana, graduated as valedictorian of his 1923 high school class, and attended Bowdoin College in Maine and the Columbia School of Journalism. He was a Nieman Fellow at Harvard. He taught at Tulane, wrote for the *New Orleans Item-Tribune* and both United Press and the Associated Press.

His influence began in earnest in 1932, when he and his wife, the former Betty Werlein, founded the *Hammond Daily Courier*. The *Courier* and the Carters, despite their support of the Democratic Party, became fierce critics of Louisiana governor Huey Long. After moving to Greenville in 1939 and launching the *Delta Democrat-Times*, Carter's editorials won him a Pulitzer Prize in 1946, prompting Senator Theodore G. Bilbo, a member of the Ku Klux Klan who believed in "the physical separation of the races," to say, "No self-respecting Southern white man would accept a prize given by a bunch of nigger-loving, Yankeefied communists for editorials advocating the mongrelization of the race."

A great deal of attention came to Carter for his editorials about the ill treatment of Japanese American soldiers (Nisei) returning from World War II. No less important were his editorials about the social injustice he observed in his native South; he became known as the "Spokesman of the New South." When *Look* magazine published his article about the White Citizens' Council, one or more members of the Mississippi House of Representatives labeled it a "willful lie by a nigger-loving editor." By a vote of 89 to 19, the Mississippi House resolved him to be a liar.

Hodding Carter weighed in with authority on numerous other issues, from his years-earlier opposition to the Munich Conference that strengthened Hitler's hand to his unabashed support of the

Kennedy brothers. It is always difficult to verify such stories, but it is said that Carter punched a passenger in the mouth on an airplane shortly after JFK was assassinated when the man bragged, "Well, we got that son of a bitch, didn't we?"

◆

I was no Amon Giles Carter as a contributor to life in the city of my birth, but I was the 1972 president of the San Antonio Chamber of Commerce during a period of important growth in our city. As the city was the largest in the state without a four-year public university, I joined other community leaders in urging the Texas legislature to establish the University of Texas at San Antonio. Lieutenant Governor Ben Barnes cut in half the gavel he used in proclaiming the bill creating UTSA passed by the Texas Senate, and gave half to me and half to State Senator Frank Lombardino, sponsor of the creating legislation.

The civic undertaking generating great public thanks to me—and no small amount of criticism—occurred after my term as Chamber president ended. My successor, a man named Pat Legan, who became one of San Antonio's most effective and dedicated community leaders, asked me to head a task force to solve one of the city's most annoying and crippling problems.

Access to the San Antonio airport was horrid, often requiring travel in bumper-to-bumper traffic on interior streets through the city's most active and fastest growing residential and business sections. Led by a powerful and dedicated mayor, Walter W. McAllister, city, state, and federal authorities fashioned a plan for the North Expressway (today known as the McAllister Freeway), a direct shot that would take less than an hour from almost anywhere in the city to get to the airport. Not so incidentally, it would reduce the daily frustration of commuters with homes in the fastest-growing residential areas north of the city.

As early as 1961, there were conservationists—funded in part by wealthy San Antonians who didn't want the freeway near their homes—who tried to stop the project. The courts rejected their suit to halt the project in its entirety but did stop construction of the center section, which would have "taken" a small number of acres of Brackenridge and Olmos Parks; those lost acres were the core issue for the conservationists. The city fathers and an overwhelming majority of San Antonians, who had voted two to one to approve the bond issue, thought the saving of an estimated 35,000 gallons of gasoline daily, not to mention precious hours wasted in automobiles, was more environmentally friendly than a few acres of parkland that could easily be replaced with other parkland. By 1972, after a torturous legal battle, the north and south sections had been built . . . but not the center section.

Like most San Antonians, I saw this as an almost unbelievable example of human folly: Some $11 million—more than $66 million in today's dollars—had been spent on the beginning and ending sections of a freeway left to deteriorate while a legal maneuver forced San Antonians to crawl to the airport and to their northeast and northwest San Antonio homes, wasting time and gasoline.

Legan and I formed a task force that included a distinguished and popular former district attorney, a politically well-connected automobile dealer, at least one other former Chamber president, and a number of other local heavyweights. We went to work on a legislative solution, as it appeared obvious this matter wasn't about to get satisfactorily resolved in the courts. We started with our local and regional representatives in Congress and our two United States senators, John Tower (who was, believe it or not, the first Republican senator from "red state" Texas since Reconstruction), and LBJ- and John Connally–backed Democratic senator Lloyd Bentsen, who is best remembered for the famous 1988 debate rebuff of VP candidate Dan Quayle, "I knew Jack Kennedy. Jack Kennedy was a friend of mine. Senator, you're no Jack Kennedy."

We succeeded in getting legislation passed and freed the freeway. Tower, who likely didn't have a large following among the conservationist elite, never mentioned it, but my friend Senator Bentsen gave me a piece of his mind because of the extent to which the Sierra Club and others in the movement came down on him. I got a few hits myself, including a piece on *60 Minutes* arguing our position versus the freeway opponents.

I was then, and am now, a believer in activist conservation movements, and am confident to this day that my freeway efforts were not at odds with that ardor.

My civic activities also included a stint as chairman of the San Antonio Symphony, in training for my five years as chair of Lincoln Center for the Performing Arts more than forty years later. I also got picked, to my great surprise, by a local judge to chair a grand jury and found it to be one of the most interesting experiences of my years as publisher of the *San Antonio Light*.

One of the honest-to-God "honors" I received didn't involve raising money. I've always differentiated between so-called "honors" where citizens allow themselves to be bait for a fundraiser, which is laudatory but not truly an "honor," and recognitions that relate to something noteworthy actually accomplished by the honoree. This one wasn't a fundraiser. Although the president of the club bestowing the honor emphasized my "tireless efforts" to achieve funding by the legislature for the new University of Texas at San Antonio, I believe the freeway effort was the main reason I was awarded the 1973 Golden Deeds Award and named "San Antonio's Man of the Year" by the Exchange Club of San Antonio. Lieutenant Governor Ben Barnes, who had given me the half gavel for my UTSA efforts, showed up to participate in the ceremonies.

While the Exchange Club has honored many worthy citizens, and I would like to think I deserved some kind of recognition for the hard work on the freeway, the Man of the Year stuff was a bit overblown. And I strongly believe not much of this would have been possible without the fact that I was publisher of the *San Antonio Light*, and if my bosses at Hearst, primarily G. O. Markuson and Frank Massi, had not only permitted but applauded my activism.

◆

I had a good run as a local publisher, but there were times when I felt at risk on multiple levels. At economic risk during the 1973–1974 recession. At both economic and reputational risk because of a brief walkout by the mailers union, the only labor strike during my tenure at the *Light*. And then there was a very different kind of risk; just thinking and writing about it brings a cold sweat despite the fact that it was forty-five years ago.

In 1973 there was an increased awareness of illicit drug activity in the area, and we were writing about it, focusing specifically on Federico (Fred) Gómez Carrasco, an American-born drug baron of Mexican descent who operated in Texas from his "headquarters" in Nuevo Laredo, just across the border. Before dawn on April 8, 1973, Agapito Ruiz, forty-six, and Roy Castaño, thirty-two, were killed in a "gang-style execution." Because of their association with Carrasco, it was assumed that Carrasco, members of his drug army, or competing drug ringleaders had ordered the murders. Two months later, two more Carrasco associates were killed. It seemed logical that they, too, had run afoul of the drug king.

That November two highly regarded reporters on our staff—Peter Franklin, a veteran, and Stryker McGuire, an enterprising twenty-six-year-old—were developing a story about a witness who contended that two "dirty" local police officers had "executed" these drug operatives and tried to lay the blame on Carrasco. What they learned: Detective Lieutenant David Flores had led a six-month investigation into the killings and had enlisted the support of San Antonio City Councilman/Mayor Charles Becker, a longtime friend of mine and, as the owner of Handy Andy supermarkets, a large advertiser. By this time, Becker was no friend of our newspaper; in the mayoral election earlier that year, we had endorsed his popular, Good Government League–backed opponent, Roy Barrera, who would have been the first Hispanic mayor in more than twenty years. Becker had had a few choice things to say about his old "friend" Frank Bennack.

I generally had no direct involvement in the investigative pieces of our staff, unless whatever they were working on needed my support or engagement by our lawyers. But high-level police corruption and murder were being alleged here, and the mayor's active engagement said to me that I'd better keep a close eye on this one. Not only were Franklin and McGuire working the story all day every day, much of the work was taking place at night. I got in the habit of showing up in the newsroom at night with Church's fried chicken or Jim's barbecue for the reporters and their editors.

The editors, including our top editor, William Bellamy, were satisfied that Franklin and McGuire's story was ready to go by Saturday, November 24, 1973. The Sunday, November 25, edition of the *Light* was headlined "Witness Says Cops Killed 2," and the entire front page was devoted to the story of the "eyewitness," the pledge of Mayor Becker that an "all-out probe" would be underway based on the account of what Franklin and McGuire had been told by their mystery witness. Down the left-hand column of the *Light* front page was an editorial urging police authorities to get to the bottom of this alleged corruption and praising the active involvement of Mayor Becker and the work of Detective Flores. Inside the main section another full page of stories contained a drawing depicting the "crime scene" and a lengthy history of the Carrasco drug operation.

The day after we broke the story, the rival *San Antonio Express* headlined "Probe Slaps PD." It described the Becker-Flores investigation in terms similar to our stories but contended that the "Premature Disclosure Jeopardizes Investigation," a clear slap at our story. From that day, the two papers were in a race. Every day seemed to bring new developments.

On the second or third day, the newsroom got word that if we continued to pursue the story, the "health" of *Light* leadership, clearly including me, might be at risk. We published the threat. I got the message and enlisted Morrie Cotton, our general manager, to stay in my home with my wife and daughters as I continued my nightly delivery of fried chicken and daily support of our journalists.

I have to admit, I was damned afraid.

After getting home from my chicken run one night, and shortly after I had fallen asleep, the phone rang. On the other end of the phone was one of our guys telling me that federal agents had busted Daniel Jaramillo—the witness in the Franklin and McGuire stories—after he attempted to sell them six pounds of heroin. My God, had we been duped?

The story didn't end for a long time. In some respects, it never ended. The City Council backed the mayor in his efforts to bring the federal government into the probe while the police department leadership denied there was any corruption and vowed to get to the bottom of these allegations. The local district attorney impaneled a grand jury, even though William Sessions, the U.S. attorney for the Western District of Texas (and, later, director of the FBI), refused to do so. The county grand jury failed to issue indictments. One of the officers took and "passed" a polygraph test.

The story peaked again when it was alleged that Louisiana Mafia boss Carlos Marcello had connections to Carrasco and was regularly making "business trips" to San Antonio. The *San Antonio Express* published allegations that Carrasco was getting "country club" treatment in the county jail, including a "Thanksgiving Feast" with his family. According to the medical examiner, security forces killed Carrasco after he took a number of hostages in an attempted escape from the state prison at Huntsville.

One or both of the accused policemen threatened to sue the mayor for defamation because he disclosed their identities to the local press.

Peter Franklin, our lead reporter on the story, went on, as Diana Britt Franklin, to write a dozen books, including *The Good-Bye*

Door, which won three literary awards and which the Discovery Channel filmed as a six-part series titled *Deadly Women*. Franklin also authored a syndicated food column for Universal Press Syndicate. Franklin's colleague, Stryker McGuire, became a correspondent, bureau chief, editor, and contributing editor at *Newsweek*, followed by a stint in London for Bloomberg.

It's possible that the worst events alleged by the mayor and Detective Flores actually took place and the guilty participants got away scot-free. Or that the entire episode was mischaracterized and brought into the public arena because of the support of the mayor and his associates, and the policemen were totally innocent, and it was, in fact, all Carrasco's doing.

Good journalists—and we had them—double-check and triple-check. But sometimes sorting out conflicting evidence to find the truth can be elusive even in the best-managed newsrooms.

CHAPTER 5

On the Road

I n September 1974, Frank Massi, who at the time was president and CEO of Hearst, and John R. Miller, then executive vice president, came to San Antonio with their wives and, while having dinner in my home with Luella and our five girls, asked me to accept the appointment as general manager of the Hearst Newspapers. Luella's expression told me it was all right to accept.

I had a conflict. New York wanted me to move to New York immediately. But I had commitments I wanted to honor in San Antonio. And it wasn't just the business conflict. It was true that I had two daughters in college who wouldn't be inconvenienced by our move, but I had three younger girls in local schools who would.

At the paper we were in a delicate situation. Rupert Murdoch had recently acquired the *Express-News*, bringing a much tougher competitive environment. We were still ahead in the local newspaper war, but it was definitely a war. Competitive newspaper markets were disappearing right and left. Between 1970 and 1990, afternoon newspapers in the U.S. declined from about 1,500 to just north of a thousand, and most of those were in smaller markets where only one newspaper was published. In Texas, only four large cities—Houston, Dallas, San Antonio, and El Paso—supported competitive newspapers. Sadly, none of the four does today.

In consultation with Massi and Miller, it was decided that we'd appoint Bill Bellamy, executive editor of the *Light* and the most respected and experienced member of my team, to succeed me as publisher. My family and I would stay in San Antonio until school was out. Well, my family would—until the summer, I would travel to our other newspapers, starting like tomorrow, because some of them, notably the *Seattle Post-Intelligencer* and the *Los Angeles Herald Examiner*, faced severe immediate challenges and were losing a fair amount of money. There was also concern about the *Baltimore News American*, which was marginally profitable. The *Boston Herald* was in a moderate loss position and trending down. Besides my *San Antonio Light*, only two were solidly profitable: Albany, where Hearst had merged its afternoon *Knickerbocker News* into its *Times Union*, and San Francisco, where our *San Francisco Examiner* had a joint operating agreement with the larger morning *Chronicle*.

The nine months that I traveled turned out to be valuable because I had the chance to work with our local newspaper publishers and their teams without the distraction of having to integrate my activities into the home office corporate environment of New York. That experience taught me another valuable lesson: When you ask somebody to take on a tough job, insulate them from as many distractions as possible so they can devote themselves full-time to the tasks at hand. Focus is an indispensable ingredient in problem solving, and corporate structural neatness can be easily overrated.

◆

Being the publisher and chief executive of your hometown newspaper is, as I've said, about as good as work can get. The old joke—"I am actually getting paid for this"—applies to a job like that.

In San Antonio I lived fifteen minutes from my office. The community engagement and social privileges added greatly to the pleasures of my job. And the competition from the other media, particularly from the other newspapers, was an engaging daily challenge.

Now I was living in New Canaan, Connecticut, 50.1 miles from my midtown Manhattan office. As I certainly didn't have a driver in those days, the only practical way to get there and back was the Metro-North train. That was an hour-and-six-minute ride. (Shortly after moving to New Canaan we attended a community celebration where we learned that the train to New York in 1975 took one hour and six minutes, which is exactly as long as the trip took in 1900.)

This commute made for a difficult transition that my Texas friends wouldn't have believed I could tolerate. The annoyance wasn't the time. It was the schedule. The last direct train to New Canaan left Grand Central Terminal at 6:10 p.m. The next train took a lot longer because it required a transfer in Stamford to the New Canaan shuttle. My business life was so challenging and demanding that two days a week, and sometimes more, I'd miss that damned 6:10 and have to listen to the truly chilly voice(s) from home when I called to announce I wouldn't be there for a 7:30 family dinner. To remind myself of the inconvenience, I saved the monthly commuter passes every month for all of the eight years I made that daily train ride.

Then there was the travel. Not to complain, just to acknowledge: Those bumpy airport van rides to LaGuardia or Newark, shuttle flights to Boston, and cross-country flights to Seattle also ate hours I would have preferred to spend near printer's ink.

The challenges only started there. When I reported for duty I was turned over to a fellow named Jim Lusnar, a magazine company employee who, among other duties, looked after the head-quarters building. Lusnar was to set me up with an appropriate office. The office he showed me wasn't a broom closet, but it could have been. In a split second I couldn't decide whether to pass out or head for the airport to go back to San Antonio.

John Miller saved the day by assigning me a larger office down the hall from his own. He explained that there was somewhat of a cultural Blues and Grays division—as in the Civil War—at the Eighth Avenue Hearst headquarters building because of "under-standable" competition between the newspaper management and the magazine management. That was something else I could think about fixing.

◆

In 1974 and 1975, my priority was to jump-start a recovery in our "DNA business"—newspapers—and leave the more far-reaching corporate strategy to my bosses. My assignment in those first nine months was narrow: deal with the problems so as to free up finan-cial resources to expand into new newspaper markets where we could own the leaders. In less formal language: rebuild the Hearst newspaper company.

One solution was collaboration. We launched the process that ultimately led to a successful negotiation to join our *Seattle Post-Intelligencer* with the stronger *Seattle Times* through what is known as a JOA, or joint operating agreement. JOAs were the product of a 1970 federal law enacted during the Richard Nixon administration designed to extend the life of struggling newspapers. The law, the Newspaper Preservation Act, permitted competitive newspapers to combine production, distribution, and business operations, including the sale of advertising, which might otherwise be illegal under antitrust laws, so long as the papers maintained fully competing editorial voices. A dozen or so such combinations were formed across the country. That agreement added more than twenty years to the life of the *Post-Intelligencer* and provided Seattle with newspaper editorial competition long beyond the time when most second newspapers were disappearing altogether. An online version of the *PI*, as the *Post-Intelligencer* has always been known, continues today.

Another solution was fresh talent. I assembled an all-star cast. I recruited Reg Murphy from the *Atlanta Constitution* and *Journal* to San Francisco. Jim Bellows, a star editor at the *Los Angeles Times*, the old *New York Herald Tribune*, and, that year, editor of the resurgent *Washington Star*, came to the *Los Angeles Herald Examiner* and brought in Mary Anne Dolan. She would eventually succeed him as the newspaper's top editor, one of the first women to be the top editor of a major market newspaper. At thirty-five, she surely was among the youngest. Robert Bergenheim, from the *Christian Science Monitor*, became publisher of the *Boston Herald*. Virgil Fassio moved from the *Chicago Tribune* to the *Seattle Post-Intelligencer*. Harry Rosenfeld, an assistant managing editor at the *Washington Post* who had been a key player in the *Post*'s coverage of Watergate, joined us to edit the combined papers in Albany. There were others worthy of mention; I apologize for my inability to include all who joined what felt very much like a crusade.

The combination of top editorial talent with a strong publisher resulted, most dramatically early on, in a favorable bounce in the financial performance of the *Boston Herald* from 1975 to 1977; it didn't last and we ultimately sold that newspaper to Rupert Murdoch. Although the Murdoch organization no longer owns the *Herald*, it continues to be published, offering an alternative to the historically powerful *Boston Globe.*

A third solution was heartache. It quickly became clear to me that we would have to close some money losers. It was a sad truth, but the media world had changed—almost every American city but one or two was destined to become a one-newspaper town.

Despite my focus on the future of our newspapers, my most urgent private conclusion was that if Hearst didn't establish a significant electronic presence—that is: in television—its future would never look like the past, when it was among the most powerful media entities in the country. We didn't begin that pivot in earnest until well after I reported to Hearst's New York headquarters—and, in fact, not until 1978, when John Miller made the decision to turn the Company over to me with the inspiring message that I would do things with the Company that he couldn't. Even before he stepped down, Miller built on the goodwill he had established and the better balance sheet he had helped quarterback to give me the go-ahead to make the first Hearst acquisition of a new business in a new market since 1958. And it was not a signal of change in direction. It was a newspaper: the midsize *Midland Reporter Telegram*, in the center of the Texas oil patch, a property sought after by many large publishing organizations. That transaction helped solidify support for expansion in general, particularly among Hearst Family members.

Because it was the first step in building the new Hearst, and because it created dramas of its own, some details about the Midland acquisition merit retelling. It began on the only trip I ever made to Los Angeles without a suitcase. I had decided I could get my L.A. business done that day by taking the early flight and returning on the dreaded "red-eye" the same night.

Taking the red-eye back to New York is now, and was then, a capital bad idea. You may think you're saving a day but you're also sacrificing your ability to think and perform at peak level. It took me years to understand that. Today it has to be a matter of life and death for me to take a red-eye. It isn't how many hours you're on the job that matters, it's how awake and creative you are.

Richard J. V. Johnson, president of the *Houston Chronicle* and a Texas pal who would later work for us at Hearst when we acquired the *Chronicle*, called me in Los Angeles during that turnaround day. He told me that the *Midland Reporter Telegram* was about to be sold, and as he knew I wanted to get Hearst into an acquisition mode, he suggested that I'd better throw our hat in the ring before Gannett, Newhouse, Times Mirror, and other competitors submitted their bids.

I scrubbed my plan to return to New York and flew to Midland. As I didn't have a suitcase I'm not sure what the reception desk at the Midland Hilton thought I was up to, but I do know that Johnson was absolutely right about the competition. Potential acquirers were gathering as if it were a newspaper convention. It was as if you could ask at the front desk what room Mr. Al Neuharth, the legendary CEO of Gannett, was in—and get an answer.

When I finally met Mrs. James Allison Sr., the paper's principal owner, she said, "Glad to meet you, Mr. Batten." She had confused me with the CEO of another interested newspaper and broadcast company, Landmark Communications. Mrs. Allison also told me that the only thing she knew about Hearst was that we had started the Spanish-American War.

On the second day in Midland I visited the local men's store and bought underwear and a new shirt. By the weekend I was discarding my New York business suit and tie and buying sports clothes so as to look a bit more like the people I was dealing with. (For years I referred to a sport coat and pair of slacks that I really liked as my "Midland" wardrobe.)

John Miller, still CEO of Hearst, flew in to help me close the deal. Miller had an injured right foot that required him to wear a tennis shoe with the toe cut out. Wagging that tennis shoe became a signal—when he started swinging it, he was advising me that it was time to cut off negotiations, slow down, and say we might have to pull out if we didn't get a deal we could afford. I think it helped.

Harvey Lipton was Hearst's general counsel and the most conservative of lawyers. He became one of my closest and wisest allies during my CEO tenure and made a huge contribution to the new Hearst along with becoming a warm personal friend. Harvey was an Orthodox Jew who kept kosher. Largely for that reason—but also because he claimed to have only one pair of pajamas—he hated to travel and rarely did. We finally convinced Lipton that this was the real thing and he needed to join us. There was no room at the Midland Hilton, so we made reservations for him at a motel. After he checked in, we told him we thought it might be the only whorehouse in Midland. He acted as if he believed us, ate nothing but tuna fish the entire time he was there, and never smiled during the entire drama of getting the deal done.

Successfully completing the negotiations for the purchase of the Midland newspaper and its smaller sister daily in Plainview, which came with the transaction, was followed by an event I value even more than beating out the competitive bidders. John Miller was stepping down the next month. Following a Hearst tradition, he was hosting a major party for his successor at the Metropolitan Club in New York. That party was scheduled for the Saturday night of the week we had spent in Midland. In attendance from around the country, and beyond: the publishers and editors of Hearst magazines and newspapers, television and radio station managers, senior corporate staff officers, heads of all the other Hearst businesses—King Features Syndicate, Avon Books, the western real estate, ranching, and timber divisions—and, of course, a sizable contingent of Hearst Family members. And spouses.

The work in Midland kept us there until Saturday morning. We hastily boarded a rarely used charter aircraft and headed for Teterboro, New Jersey. There was heavy traffic. The plane, low enough on fuel for the pilots to mention it, had to wait and wait for clearance to land. We barely got into Manhattan in time to get tuxedos on and join the guests at the Metropolitan Club.

That evening is especially meaningful to me because, in addition to Luella and my daughters, Miller had arranged for my father and stepmother to be in attendance. It was Dad's first trip outside Texas. The pride he exhibited that night and the hospitality shown him by my Hearst colleagues still inspires a chill of excitement and a Texas-size smile.

CHAPTER 6

The Genius of the Founder

I f you look only at my résumé, it would appear as if my career was rocket-powered almost as soon as I arrived in New York. In fact, it was. But beyond whatever talent and energy I brought to my new job, there was also what is often the most critical factor of all—luck. If ever someone was in the right place at the right time, I was that man.

The mentoring and support of John Miller, who had succeeded Massi as CEO in 1975, rivaled the enormous help I had gotten from B. J. Horner. It was as if he had already decided what the next steps were going to be for Hearst leadership. What I didn't know was that Miller had promised his wife he would retire on his sixty-fifth birthday in January of 1979, and he was committed to having a successor in place to make that possible.

At the December 1975 board meeting—less than a year after I moved to New York—Miller orchestrated my election as executive vice president, effectively COO, of the entire company, although we didn't yet use that title. I quickly bonded with Gilbert C. Maurer, who had been recruited in 1973 as vice president of the Motor Division of Hearst Magazines but had quickly been advanced by

Miller to the presidency of the entire magazine division. With good reason: After Harvard Business School, Gil had spent nineteen years in substantive roles at Cowles Communications. Now he was making a big difference in the fortunes of Hearst magazines. Gil opened up the magazine company to me without hesitation, ending the stifling Blues and Grays legacy and launching our indispensable forty-plus-year partnership. I replaced myself as general manager of the Hearst Newspapers with Robert J. Danzig, the charismatic young publisher of the Albany newspapers, who started as a copy boy and whose career in New York's capital city appeared a great deal like my own in San Antonio.

One impetus for my relatively quick upgrade was that John Miller wanted help with the task of repaying the debt that had been incurred for the purchase of Hearst common stock at a cost of $136 million from the two Hearst Foundations. That transaction—we refer to it as the "recapitalization"—had been mandated by the Tax Reform Act of 1969. An even greater impetus was Miller's commitment to building the platform for the new Hearst Corporation we both envisioned. He didn't think the acquisition program that would take the company to the next level was possible yet—Hearst first had to pay down its debt and assemble a war chest. That could have been a singularly difficult goal but, happily, two realities over which we had no control or influence helped set the table for future success.

The first had to do with the unusual structure William Randolph Hearst put in place in a rather remarkable will and testamentary plan. Many, maybe even most, family companies are simply passed along from generation to generation. The outcomes vary, but we've seen that companies using that traditional method frequently tend not to maintain the success achieved by their genius founders.

The Brits have a saying that illustrates what too often happens to family businesses: "clogs to clogs in three generations." It's not known if W. R. Hearst, who was somewhat of an Anglophile, or the skilled advisers who collaborated with him on his testamentary plan had that in mind. We do know that he wanted to do everything he could to ensure that the company he almost lost during the Depression would survive as deep into the future as possible.

W. R. Hearst's way of dealing with that was to establish a trust—the Hearst Family Trust—that would remain in effect until "the death of the last survivor of decedent's sons and grandchildren living at the time of decedent's death." The meaning of that provision in nonlegal terms is that the trust would expire after the death of every descendant of Mr. Hearst who had been alive at the time of his death in 1951. That date was far in the future at the time the trust was created; it's now predicted by actuaries that the last of the heirs born prior to his death will have died by around 2041 or a few years later. Additionally, Mr. Hearst made eight of his most trusted business associates and his five sons the trustees of the trust for their lifetimes, in effect giving the "professionals" eight-to-five control of the company until the trust's expiration. The trustees to succeed that original group, of which I am one, would be appointed by surviving trustees, always in the ratio of eight nonfamily members to five members of his family. The founder wanted his family to be involved but clearly envisioned longer and more robust success for a company managed by professionals. Also, significantly, he left all nonvoting common stock except one hundred shares to the two charitable foundations.

I've known and served with four of Mr. Hearst's five sons and most of their descendants. I valued their wisdom and support throughout my tenure as CEO, and right up to the present day. William R. Hearst Jr., W.R.'s second son and namesake, was a cheerleader second to none for my administration and me. Randolph A. Hearst, another of W.R.'s sons, and Mr. Hearst's grandsons, George R. Hearst Jr. and William R. Hearst III, served as chairs of our board during my days at the helm. I never saw any resentment that the testator didn't leave direct ownership and control in their hands. To the contrary, with rare exception, they showed great enthusiasm for the way the founder's plan had worked out.

◆

The second reality that contributed to our success—and, in a major way to the well-being of Hearst Family members—was the Tax Reform Act of 1969; it required the reduction from 99 percent to no more than 20 percent of the Hearst Corporation common stock be held by the Hearst Foundations. That legislation made it illegal for a private foundation to own more than 2 percent of the voting stock of a company or, alternatively, more than 20 percent of nonvoting stock. Theoretically any willing buyer could have acquired the stock, but because of voting restrictions on the stock Hearst was likely to be the only buyer willing to pay a fair price. As the logical buyer for that stock, the Hearst trustees scraped together all the cash on hand, borrowed what seemed like a huge amount of money, and bought back the 99 percent of common stock in the Foundations. Because of their oversight of nonprofit organizations, including foundations, the attorneys general of New York and California had to bless the transaction. The courts in both states approved it, and the stock was deposited in the Family Trust. With no further requirement to pay dividends to the Foundations, the Company could use its earnings to invest in growing the Hearst Corporation and for paying appropriate dividends to the Hearst Family.

The Foundations also fared spectacularly well. The corporation paid $136 million—about $700 million in today's dollars—to the Foundations. Since 1974 the Foundations have given about $1.2 billion to worthy charities; current resources are worth about $1.1 billion.

W.R.'s ingenious structure and the serendipitous passage of the Tax Reform Act of 1969 gave Hearst magical, once-in-a-lifetime opportunities. But opportunity on its own doesn't create success. Credit a prudent investment strategy, smart acquisitions, and successful launches of new products that followed. Without that great work orchestrated by scores of skillful managers and creative talents, W.R.'s succession plan and the tax-imposed opportunity would have meant little or nothing.

◆

Yes, yes, you say, but we've all seen *Citizen Kane*. We've read about the Hearsts' fabulous wealth, their larger-than-life personalities, the kidnapping of Patty Hearst—and about their media company, managed by true believers in the church of newspapers, the medium they dominated for so long. Yes, William Randolph Hearst's testamentary plan made his family colleagues with the company's professional managers rather than autocratic rulers, and those professional managers transformed the very DNA of the enterprise, but still . . .

There is no "but still." William Randolph Hearst's testamentary plan was pure genius. And the Hearsts—especially the two sons and two grandsons who served as chairmen on my watch as CEO—contributed mightily to making that plan work and my tenure a success. William Randolph Hearst Jr., to whom I had expressed my aspirations seven years earlier in our San Antonio discussion, had relinquished his chairman's title to his brother Randolph by the time I moved to New York. Bill had taken the title chairman of the executive committee. By the time I was elected president and CEO three years later, Bill had reached his seventies but was still very much the family's eminence grise—a formidable presence in every way.

Bill began his Hearst career as a teenager, working in the summer as a lowly "flyboy"—a pressroom apprentice who literally caught bundles of newspapers as they came off the presses—at the *New York Mirror*. He left college to work for the *New York American* as a police reporter. By 1936, when he was just twenty-eight, he became its publisher. He didn't have an easy time there. He had the title, but he also had a father, and William Randolph Hearst couldn't step back from commenting.

Bill was a war correspondent in World War II. And then, in 1955, he had his greatest success as a journalist: With two colleagues, Frank Conniff and Joseph Kingsbury-Smith, Bill went to the Soviet Union to interview the country's leaders. He was especially impressed by Nikita S. Khrushchev, and on his return advised President Dwight Eisenhower that Khrushchev was going to rise to greater prominence. The following year he and his colleagues shared the Pulitzer Prize for international reporting; typical of Bill, he said his colleagues deserved it more. Journalism was oxygen to him; he wrote a weekly "Editor's Report" column for Hearst papers right up to his death in 1993.

"I lived in my father's shadow all my life," he said. Two shadows, really. William Randolph Hearst Sr. cast large shadows, one of them unreal. Yes, he built an empire. And San Simeon, probably the greatest real estate extravaganza built outside a film set. But for most people the elder Hearst's most enduring image is that of a mythic fictional tragedy—as Charles Foster Kane in Orson Welles's *Citizen Kane*, one of the greatest American movies. As for San Simeon, its reality is much different now—it's owned by the state of California.

Nobody cheered me more than Bill. He was intensely proud to be his father's son and wanted more than anything for the company to prosper. Every acquisition over the fourteen years I was CEO until his death, every launch of a new product, every recruitment of new talent—his reaction was the same: great enthusiasm.

There were a few episodes I might have preferred to change a bit. To be more accurate: one episode, repeated often. It had to do with Bill's calling me at home many Sunday mornings because he "didn't want to bother me while I was working." His comments and questions were almost always constructive, supportive, and punctuated with Bill's delightful brand of humor.

Still, it was Sunday morning.

I can't speak of Bill without speaking of Austine, his wife for forty-three years. She was responsible for one of the two statements made to me, or about me, by a Hearst Family member that I value most highly after more than a half century of living with them. At a party at the Hearsts' home in South Salem, New York, as the host of a large assemblage of friends, family, and Company associates, Austine, microphone in hand, spoke about her grandson Willie, specifically about giving him money to go shopping. He asked, "Where do you get your money?" In her uniquely strong and clear voice, she replied, "From Frank Bennack."

There are rewards that are even better than money, and that was one. But the other memorable statement is a bookend to the first—it's completely about money, and it was made by Austine and Bill's oldest son, the father of the inquiring grandson, and today's chairman of the board. In what may have been a weak moment, at the conclusion of a compensation committee meeting with all the members present, William Randolph Hearst III said, "Frank, I wished we had paid you more." Well, I do, too, but I have no complaints about what I actually was paid.

One of my most humorous episodes with Bill Hearst occurred before I became CEO, although I didn't find it funny when it occurred. I was COO at the time, and had worked with John Miller on an executive incentive compensation program that John wanted to implement before he stepped down. John had hired a compensation consulting firm known at that time as Towers Perrin. (Miller never got their name straight, referring to them throughout the assignment as "Lea & Perrins"—the Worcestershire sauce.) The consultants delivered their report, including an analysis of other media companies' incentive compensation practices. John and I labored over the details of the request for the compensation committee and the board to adopt. The comprehensive report was finalized and delivered to the entire board a couple of weeks before it was to be considered. The support of the Family members was critical for a variety of obvious reasons, including the absence of any conflict of interest since, unlike dividend declarations, most Family members would not be participants in the plan.

On the Monday before the meetings were to be held, Miller asked Bill and Randy to meet with us in his office to finalize our support for the plan. Five minutes into the meeting in Miller's office, it became obvious that neither Bill nor Randy had read the material.

John Miller—who seldom, if ever, raised his voice—went ballistic. A historic moment, totally out of character. But John was near the end of his tenure, and he had a strong conviction that such a program would be important to Hearst's future success in recruiting and keeping strong management. So he was not about to hide his displeasure.

I was as unhappy as John, but I didn't see myself reacting in the same way. I decided to give my fondest-of-Hearst-Family colleagues the "silent treatment," much as what happens in a family spat.

The formal consideration of the incentive compensation plan, by necessity, was postponed to a subsequent board meeting.

Randy Hearst had not yet moved permanently from San Francisco to New York. But I saw Bill almost daily when he and I weren't traveling. So he was the only Hearst to notice my silent treatment.

Eventually, Bill stuck his head in my office and asked if he could come in for a minute.

Of course I said yes.

"Baby, how long is this going to go on?" he inquired.

I couldn't suppress a hearty laugh. I had full confidence that Bill and Randy weren't actually opposed to the adoption of an incentive plan for the executives. They just hadn't read the damned documents!

Bill and I proceeded to have a rational and mutually supportive conversation, after which he said he would carefully review the plan and be prepared to support its adoption. He said he was sure Randy would do the same. And that's what happened.

◆

Randy and I became quite close. During the years up until 1996 when he left the chairman's chair in favor of George Hearst Jr., we spent many hours together discussing almost every move of importance the company was considering.

Randy had a statement he regularly used: "You're going to want me in on the landing, so you need to have me in on the takeoff."

That seemed an appropriate metaphor for a guy who ferried planes for the U.S. Army Air Corps during World War II. Randy's sense of humor, including his capacity for self-deprecating humor, was both charming and disarming. He regularly said that those days he spent in the Air Corps were the most important in his life. "Because," he would say, "Pop forgot to buy the Air Corps."

The metaphor of being "in on the takeoff" was more than a reference to his own flying experience. He clearly expected that there would be no big surprises or activities of significance that hadn't been revealed to him first. He wasn't seeking to substitute his judgment for those of management. He just wanted to avoid not knowing the answer when a family member asked him about a company matter. Fair enough!

Dustups? Given our roles, it would have been impossible for us to serve together for seventeen years without a few. It would be equally impossible for me not to be responsible for at least one. I remember a time when Randy hotfooted into my office doing about twenty miles an hour. He described the issue and his unhappiness, and wanted to know why we had done whatever it was. I replied, "Randy, sometimes we are just stupid; this is one of those times." This was an occasion when I said—to myself—an oft-used Bennackism: "I was born at night, but not last night."

Not only did Randy Hearst give me an undeserved level of credit for what the company had become on my watch, he reached out to spend as much time with me as possible. He took me bird hunting, hosted dinners at his home or at a favorite Mexican restaurant. Both he and I remembered all those hours we had spent together in San Francisco after Patty had been brutally taken from her family on February 4, 1974; in some ways I think we bonded then.

As part of what I now think of as my audition to head the Hearst Newspapers, late in 1973 Frank Massi had asked me to spend some time with Randy, who was then president of the *San Francisco Examiner*, to help him determine if more could be done to elevate the performance of the afternoon and Sunday papers, which Hearst had responsibility for in the joint operating agreement. The morning paper was produced by the *San Francisco Chronicle*. I had traveled to San Francisco several times, and Randy and I were in regular contact around the time Patty was kidnapped.

Among many strong recollections I have about that period is the bizarre kidnapping of *Atlanta Constitution* editor Reg Murphy on February 20, 1974, just two weeks after the Patty Hearst abduction. Some observers, me included, were of the opinion that the two kidnapping incidents might represent a planned pattern of attacks on newspaper-related targets. As it turned out, they weren't related, but I remember the local FBI chief showing up at my San Antonio office to advise me to vary the route I took home and to avoid predictable patterns in my life in case the bad guys had targeted more newspaper personnel. The complete motive of the Murphy abduction was never understood, but his newspaper paid a $700,000 ransom. The kidnapper was arrested within hours and the money was recovered.

During the year Patty was held by her captors, Randy, his then wife and Patty's mother, Catherine, and I often had dinner in San Francisco or Hillsborough when I was visiting the paper in San Francisco. More than once an FBI agent joined us. As a father of five daughters, observing the ordeal of the Hearst Family and Patty was painful in the extreme.

Years later Patty and her delightful husband, Bernie Shaw, became our friends and Bernie my colleague as he undertook the responsibility for the Company's security force. Luella and I served as godparents for the Shaws' second daughter, Lydia Marie.

I've seldom encountered in business a more understated, gentle, generous, and conscientious human being than Randy Hearst. We shared responsibility at the top of the corporation for seventeen years, but our friendship endured for more than three decades. I genuinely enjoyed our journey together. Any negatives were not of his making.

When Randy stepped down as chairman, there was considerable discussion around whether, as in most large companies, I should take the chairman's title along with being CEO. Hearst had actually had more than one chairman in the past who wasn't a family member. And I could see the merit of that, as almost all the CEOs I was dealing with were both.

I thought about it, discussed it with a number of the trustees and key board members, and decided that the modern tradition that began with Bill Hearst's chairmanship was important to the Family and ought to be continued. Besides, the absence of the chairman's title wasn't holding me back. I always believed the only justification of title inflation is if it helps you perform your job better.

◆

George Hearst Jr., W.R. Hearst's eldest grandson, and I met when we were both local publishers. I had it easier—just weeks after I became publisher in San Antonio, George, who was publisher of the *Los Angeles Herald Examiner*, faced a bitter strike by the newspaper unions. He called to warn me the unions had made it clear that they intended to demonstrate at—and, if they could, shut down—the other Hearst newspapers. They did show up briefly in San Antonio, but they had no appeal for our people.

George was still publisher in Los Angeles when I became general manager of the Hearst newspapers. I regularly visited him, and we hit it off. This was a guy I could relate to. Like me, he was a veteran of the Army. In addition, he had served in the Naval Air Corps in World War II. While our Army tours of duty briefly overlapped, the similarity ended there. I had only peacetime assignments. Warrant Officer George Hearst flew a helicopter during the closing days of the Korean War, delivering supplies to the front lines and evacuating the sick and wounded from the battle zone. And George was a dedicated and highly skilled horseman and an avid hunter. What Texan wouldn't have been drawn to such a kindred spirit?

By the time I joined the Hearst board in 1974, George had already served twelve of the fifty-three years he was a director. By then, a ten-year strike and the declining fortunes of afternoon newspapers had taken a heavy toll on the paper he ran. We both knew the prospects for survival weren't great, but we did everything we could to resist or delay what we feared was inevitable. And our personal chemistry and our broader interests in all things Hearst as directors somewhat softened the daily disappointment in L.A.

In 1977 George moved over to assume oversight of the Company's significant western real estate, timber, and ranching activities, and was succeeded as publisher of the *Herald Examiner* by Francis Dale, who had been publisher of the *Cincinnati Enquirer*. The *Herald Examiner*, after deep and continuing losses, and despite a period of journalistic revival under Jim Bellows and Mary Anne Dolan and an infusion of talent we authorized Dale and Bellows to recruit, closed for good on November 2, 1989. The closing headline read: "So Long, L.A."

Seven years later we elected George to the position of chairman of the board, the first of his generation to hold that position. For the next sixteen years until his death in 2012 George served as chairman. I can't express today how I felt about those sixteen years any better than I did in the painful news release penned after we lost him: "George was an enthusiastic supporter of the corporation's growth and diversification strategies. As chairman of the board, he brought his vast experience and wisdom to bear during a time of incredible growth and helped guide us through periods of enormous change. Although always calling every situation as he saw it, George was the most supportive and steadfast chairman a CEO could possibly have."

I never had more gratifying days on the job than those when he was in town for our board meetings. Regularly George and I and two or three of our closest management associates would have the most-delicious-ever *poulet* at the neighborhood French bistro Biarritz, while seriously talking business but also sharing our favorite toast: "Confusion to the Enemy"—affirming that whatever the competition ("the enemy") was planning, we would hope they were too confused to carry it out.

And I never had a worse day on the job than when Mary Lake and I flew to say goodbye to an unconscious and dying George Hearst Jr. at Stanford University Hospital. He was eighty-four. In another month he would have been the same age at death as his predecessor chairmen, Bill and Randy.

◆

There was a certain inevitability about William Randolph Hearst III, "Will," eventually following his father, uncle, and older cousin into the chairman's role. He graduated from Harvard in 1972, something his famous grandfather didn't do despite leaving heavy tracks there at the *Harvard Lampoon*. Although Will's degree was in mathematics, it was clear that, like his grandfather and father, he loved newspapers. Early in his career he worked for his uncle Randy on the *San Francisco Examiner*.

At the *Examiner* he became close pals with Larry Kramer, also a Harvard alumnus. Will and Larry worked together when they were both in their twenties, then Larry joined Will as executive editor from 1986 to 1991 during Will's tour as publisher of the *Examiner*. Kramer went on to become a gifted entrepreneur, creating the popular website MarketWatch, which he sold to CBS, and serving as president and publisher of *USA Today* and CEO of TheStreet along with deep academic engagements at Harvard and Syracuse.

Kramer gets mention here not only because he was one of many gifted contributors to Hearst on my watch but also because he and Will formed a formidable coalition under Randy's sponsorship that I had to cope with in my very early days as general manager of newspapers. I didn't feel all that much older than they were, but boy, did they have distinct views about what the modern newspaper ought to look like.

In his book, *The Hearsts: Father and Son*, Will's father dramatically makes this point: "As publisher of the *San Francisco Examiner*— the first newspaper launched by his grandfather—Will had made many changes: focusing on local and international news, assigning more features, beefing up columns on culture. And he was clearly contemplating more changes; he was remaking the *Examiner* into his own paper."

In 1975, the *Examiner*'s centennial year, Will made a promotional television commercial. The script called for him to sit in his office, with a large portrait of William Randolph Hearst on the wall behind him. The ghost of his grandfather asked, "Are you sure you know what you're doing, Will?"

There was no script for Will. He could say whatever he wanted. Will said, "Did you?"

A brilliant response, cutting the distance between then and now and voting for the importance of the now.

Was I ever that exuberant, that self-confident? I thought back, and recalled the time I made commercials for the San Antonio newspaper. An advertising client commented on one, telling my boss, Colonel B. J. Horner, "B.J., that assistant of yours is pretty cocky." Horner replied, "He has a reason to be." So maybe youth isn't entirely wasted on the young.

Will joined the Hearst Board of Directors the same day I did in 1974. Two years later, to the admiration of us all, he left the security of the Family Company and joined Jann Wenner as managing editor of a new magazine called *Outside.*

We lured him back to Hearst in 1980. He worked initially at the *Los Angeles Herald Examiner* and then effectively became one of our cable pioneers as vice president of our fledgling Hearst Cable Communications activity on the West Coast.

In 1985 I decided that Will, always extraordinarily bright and particularly good in two skill sets I value, writing and making numbers speak to you, was ready to enter the big leagues at his grandfather's company. He was then thirty-six, two years older than I had been when I became publisher in San Antonio, and ready to be editor and publisher of the *San Francisco Examiner.* That role drew him much closer to me; despite the challenges of an afternoon newspaper, his decade in that position remains among my, and I think his, fondest memories. He rejoined the Hearst Board of Directors when he returned to the Company in 1980, and has remained there ever since.

In 1995, with the understanding that he would not have to leave the board because there was no competitive conflict as there might have been with *Outside* magazine, Will again ventured out into the non-Hearst world and joined the powerhouse venture capital firm Kleiner Perkins. As a Kleiner partner, he was a cofounder of Home Network Broadband Internet Service and gained valuable experience and knowledge of the tech world, finances, and business management.

After the death of George Hearst Jr. in 2012, and prior to my stepping down as CEO for the second time in 2013, William Randolph Hearst III was elected chairman of the board. My successor, Steve Swartz, and our entire board have felt as I do: Will has brought wisdom, humor, support, and industry knowledge to the position. He has more than justified the inevitability of his rising to that post.

While the four board chairmen deserve special treatment in any story of my life and career, other Family members have supported me beyond what I probably actually deserved. They value their privacy, so I will salute and express my thanks to David, Phoebe, Bunky, Millicent, Gina, Austin, George III, Steve, Annisa, Lisa, Samia, and Christian, all of whom served with me on the Hearst Board of Directors, and to numerous other Hearst Family members who frequently expressed their support and, importantly, told me of their pride in what the Hearst Corporation had become on my watch.

It turns out that happy families are not all alike and dysfunctional families are not all miserable. Families, like life, are complicated, checkered, ever-changing. But over time, you can take a fair portrait. The picture I have of the Hearst Family is that it works. Indeed, it works very well.

CHAPTER 7

Okay, Now You're in Charge . . .

John Miller and I had a greatly rewarding three-plus years together. He and Frank Massi had orchestrated the quick payback of the debt that we had taken on when the Company bought back the common stock held by the two Hearst Foundations. In the relatively brief forty-five months that John Miller occupied the CEO chair, Hearst became a company with a different and decidedly more progressive perspective. Along the way, he taught me the most important lesson of all: Culture is the biggest determinant of business success.

In mid-1978, Miller told me he would redeem his pledge to his wife and retire on January 20, 1979, and that I was to be his successor.

I thought, "In 1979, I'll be forty-six years old—young for a CEO. I'll believe that when I see it."

"I've taught you everything I can teach you," Miller said, "and you will do things with this company that I can't do." I think that was the most selfless statement I ever heard a senior executive say to a potential successor. He had one specific piece of advice. "Don't appoint a COO right away. Give the organization time to know your key reports well enough to support the choice you eventually make." Instead, John recommended that I appoint Benson Srere, United Press International newsman turned managing editor of *Good Housekeeping* turned general manager of King Features Syndicate, as vice president and executive assistant to the president. That turned out to be one of the best appointments I'd make; Ben was truly indispensable as I grew into my CEO responsibilities.

John Miller retired on January 20, 1979, his sixty-fifth birthday, and I succeeded him as CEO. Cancer killed him the following December, and I again lost an irreplaceable mentor and supporter. For the second time I was a business orphan of sorts, with huge new responsibilities and without the mentorship that had gotten me there in the first place.

Why was I privileged to have the support and mentoring I received from the people I have described here? Was it simply the luck of being in the right place at the right time? Was it because I exhibited a clear desire to learn and to advance? What was it that motivated a diminutive nun, a toughened World War II hero turned newspaper publisher, two sophisticated veterans of the New York corporate scene, and others, to give me more of themselves than I could ever deserve?

◆

There is no "How to Become a CEO" guide, and if there were, the only person who would benefit from it is the writer who suckered ambitious people into buying it. There are no shortcuts. There isn't even a clear path. But if I had to commend one, I'd suggest the ideal route looks something like this. Choose parents with solid, sensible values. Go to schools that prioritize learning, a work ethic, and team play. Along the way, get jobs that help you discover your strengths and interests. Look for mentors and listen closely to them. Your job and your family matter, but so does your community; be an involved citizen. Embrace each step on the ladder as if it's your last—don't look at the corner office as the brass ring.

That's pretty much how my life and career played out, right up to age forty-six, when I was tapped to be Hearst's CEO. Again, my ascent could not have been better timed. In 1979, Hearst had ten or so magazines in the United States, a small number of foreign versions of those magazine titles abroad, mostly in the U.K., eight daily newspapers, a paperback book publisher, three television stations, and AM and FM radio stations in the same markets where the TV stations were located, most of which had some earnings we could use to start acquiring and investing, and a corporate staff that shared our hopes for a bright future. All my colleagues and I had to do was lead the company into the future without destroying the past.

The day you become a CEO you get a blank slate. All the lines you've accumulated in the yearbook of life no longer matter. Your mentors can't help you—indeed, mine were dead or would die soon. Your board of directors is eager for you to succeed but unsentimental about replacing you if you fail. You're like an actor at the moment the script calls for you to stand alone in the spotlight. Every asset and weakness is exposed.

One other factor: Behind you is a library of business articles and CEO books. They dispense contradictory wisdom, but they tend to agree on one thing: Hit the ground running and put some quick victories on the scoreboard. Many invoke "100 days" as a metric. If the management pundits are right, you not only have to do something newsworthy, you have to do it against a ticking clock.

Perhaps those mantras work . . . somewhere. But in 1979, Hearst was a special situation. As I've noted, until the Midland newspaper the company had not made an acquisition of a new business since 1958, in part because of the memory of the company's near-demise during the Depression, in part because of its innate conservatism. Condé Nast, our major competitor in magazines, was known for its open checkbook. At Hearst, it was said, we "threw our nickels around like manhole covers."

I remember when the *San Antonio Light* was building a new headquarters. A construction expert from a Hearst newspaper in California came to oversee the project. A day of studying the figures led to a sleepless night. What happened? "I think the contractor is going to make a profit on this job," he reported, aghast.

◆

As CEO, an early priority was novel for Hearst, and a paradox. In a company as historically tight as Hearst, I needed to make a high-profile acquisition—and to make it, completely against the company's history and reputation, at full price.

I had three sound reasons. An acquisition at full price is an announcement to other companies: We're in the market; if you have something good you want to sell, call us. It's also an announcement to talent: Rethink your view of Hearst, because we are ambitious and inventive, and you just might like to work here. Finally, it's a pep talk for our employees: We're on the move.

It was clear to me that television would be the dominant medium of the immediate future, and three television stations and six radio stations didn't represent an electronic future. We needed a bit more than that. And for this cash-strapped company to get there, we'd have to close some papers—especially some increasingly unprofitable big-city afternoon papers.

At the same time, there were some morning papers we'd be smart to buy. Midland was a start. We acquired television stations in Dayton and Kansas City.

After the first acquisitions, we did something equally out of character for Hearst. To describe what a modern Hearst was and what we were doing, we took out full-page ads in a number of important publications, in addition to running them in our own papers. These ads were an arrow to the future, a statement of ambition, determination, and confidence.

The negotiation for the Dayton, Ohio, TV station was my first encounter with one of the most storied business leaders of our time. Warren Buffett, then about fifty years old and not nearly as well-known as he is today, had engineered the purchase of television station WDTN-TV in Dayton as an investment for the endowment of Grinnell, a small liberal arts college in Iowa, where he was a trustee at the time. I don't think we ever learned the exact gain realized by Grinnell in that transaction, but I believe Grinnell's capital fund had bought the station for $13 or $14 million in 1976 and sold it to us for $47 million in 1981. Not a bad return on investment.

Around that same time, for $80,000—yes, just $80,000, or

about $232,000 in today's dollars—we acquired First Databank, a pharmaceutical database company that, after a couple of small "tuck-in" acquisitions, became a more than $100 million business for us. But we lost an auction for a newspaper DuPont owned in Wilmington, Delaware, because, I always believed, one of my associates was so excited the company was expanding that he told a reporter we were bidding $60 million. Gannett outbid us by peanuts. When I called Randy Hearst, who was then chairman of our board, I apparently sounded so bad that he said, "Well, you still have the $60 million, don't you?"

Randy had lived through disappointments: the closure of newspapers in Pittsburgh, Milwaukee, Atlanta, and Fort Worth. "The hurt goes away," he told me. "It's not personal. Some things just don't work."

True, but so much of the CEO's job is acutely personal. The CEO is not just the company's public spokesman, he/she is its mission statement, walking. "A psychoanalyst talking is like playing golf on the moon," John Updike wrote. "Even a chip shot carries for miles." That's equally true for a CEO. When he/she whispers, the staff hears a shout.

CHAPTER 8

The CEO: An Operator's Guide

Deals and acquisitions make the headlines. Unnoticed things—often things that seem small and unimportant—define a culture. And in any organization, culture is everything. Here are some cultural dos and don'ts I learned by listening to mentors, watching others, swapping stories with CEOs, and, in the case of the Korean wigs—yes, Korean wigs—and Hearst Tower's architectural transparency, by unique personal experience. They're not carved in stone, but CEOs who embrace them tend, in my observation, to last longer and do better than those who re-invent the job.

1) As CEO, you're a father/mother figure. It's your job to mentor, to help your people grow. That starts with the people who have long served the company—you owe it to them to help them succeed in their jobs. Grant Tinker, whom I greatly admired, is said to have taken NBC from last place to first without firing anyone; maybe that's not correct in a strictly technical sense, but I've been told it was directionally true. When I became CEO of Hearst, I inherited a solid group of

executives, all but one homegrown. When we did import talent, we looked for superstars. Among that illustrious group: Al Sikes, the first head of our New Media and Technologies Group, who had been chairman of the Federal Communications Commission in the George H. W. Bush administration, and Cathie Black, who came to us from the Newspaper Association of America after a stint as publisher of *USA Today*.

2) Bring in new people? It's tempting. You're always hearing about the turbocharged CEO who is "driving change." An easy way to recognize that CEO: His/her new broom sweeps clean. While it's tempting to look outside for super-hires, I've come to believe that companies that rely entirely, or at least primarily, on looking elsewhere for talent face significant headwinds. The new hires have obvious issues related to the length of the learning curve. And their lack of knowledge about wins and losses in the past, or their disregard of that history, can frequently result in destructive change. Equally perilous: companies where the Holy Grail is promotion from within. Because they seldom or never violate that principle, they tend to be inappropriately satisfied with the status quo and often unaware of best practices being developed outside their four walls. Balance is the key word here. Of the twenty senior-most executives who worked with me, nine were internal promotions and eleven were recruited from the outside.

3) I'm not big on headhunters. Part of my job was to know who's out there; if we were hiring from outside Hearst, I pre-

ferred to rely on my network of friends and contacts in our business and relevant business segments to tell me who were the truly good people they knew. And when I met potential hires, I rarely asked about work success. That was assumed. The one question I had for everyone: What else do you do? Work and family—of course they matter. But if work and family are your life, you won't be successful at Hearst. We need to know about your life outside these walls and your home. Involvement in the arts? A charitable activity or passion for a book club? Anything intellectually stimulating or rewarding?

4) The optimal blend of inside and recruited talent is critical, but so is the follow-up: integration of the two classes of executives. One of the ways I worked on that was to find ways to bring executives and their spouses together whenever possible. We inaugurated an annual offsite at my Texas ranch, where our executives participated in a well-planned exercise of evaluating the status of the Company's businesses, strategy, and plans. Spouses join in the after-working-hours social calendar that includes tennis, golf, four-wheel off-road vehicle joyrides, fishing, and walking among one of the nation's most diverse exotic animal collections. The nights feature lectures from prominent governmental or literary figures such as James Baker, Robert Gates, Colin Powell, and Doris Kearns Goodwin. On the second night we're together Willie Nelson might just show up.

I have regularly tried to gather executives and spouses for nights at the Metropolitan Opera, Paley Center galas, Lincoln

Center events, and various charitable fundraisers. And there is an annual garden party at my home for executives, spouses, and their children.

Ironclad truth: Get buy-in from the spouses, and the company's culture will be more likely to promote an environment of teamwork and success than any you ever imagined. We value our relationship with the spouses, who are a splendid and impressive group of women and men, what you would expect given the best-in-class talent that makes the Company go.

5) Work with your door closed? No, you close your door as little as possible. A closed door is a signal: Something's going on that we don't want you to know about. And when you have personal news to deliver? Good news or bad, don't have that person come to you. If you're firing someone or making a significant change in his or her work life, it's best not to do it in your office—going to see that person allows you to end the meeting when you choose. But it's more a matter of respect. And not just for the individuals involved. When we hired David Carey as president of Hearst Magazines in 2010 to succeed Cathie Black and promoted Cathie to chairman, I went to the offices of the staffers who worked closest with Cathie and explained the move. A little thing? They understood. And remembered.

6) Staff conflict? I'm an activist. I like the news—good and bad— early. I respect an organizational chart, but I didn't let titles and rank get in the way when I needed to talk to people at lev-

els below my direct reports. Rigid corporate structures may look neat, but they're vastly overrated.

7) Meetings? My kids used to explain my job like this: "Daddy goes to meetings." With eight to ten direct reports, yes . . . Daddy went to meetings. As CEO, I presented at four regular and several special board meetings a year. And we had conference calls when necessary. All that is traditional. What wasn't: Group Week. During each month other than the four months when our regular board meeting was scheduled, I inaugurated a weeklong series of review meetings. I conducted separate sessions with each of our principal lines of business. Initially that meant one each day Monday through Thursday, with the group heads, their deputies, and often their operating unit executives from our Newspapers, Magazines, Broadcasting, and Books/Business Media divisions. As we grew we had to expand to more than one meeting some days to cover our newly organized business sectors, like cable networking. On Friday, I'd meet with all of them in a "joint" session of sorts where every senior executive would deliver a digest report and learn what his or her colleagues elsewhere in the Company were doing to grow and improve the Company. These sessions were amazingly useful: The preparation for them was an indispensable part of our future planning, and they ensured time-certain access to me for all our key players. My successor, Steve Swartz, has continued this tradition, and still welcomes me to the Friday sessions. If it is possible to have too much communication, I haven't yet determined when that is.

8) The new offices at Hearst Tower? Lord, we were proud of our beautiful, environmentally advanced, award-winning building. The Tower was different from even the most innovative Manhattan offices—wherever you sat, you were flooded with natural light. The design was open space; there weren't as many private offices as before. Then a few women asked me, "Where do we go to cry?" and I understood that our people needed some private space. A learning experience: There is such a thing as too much transparency.

9) Now we come to the lesson we all know—if it seems too good to be true, it generally is—but sometimes forget. This absurd episode occurred at the *San Antonio Light*, where I held regular meetings with different departments of the newspaper at 7:30 in the morning. A succession of such meetings with the advertising department management revealed that, sometime in the early 1970s, we began to publish a large volume of ads selling Korean hair wigs. I was surprised that enough wigs could be sold to justify the advertising. One particular firm seemed to be continually increasing its ad spend. I warned our ad managers that we were taking a risk of not getting paid. They showed me evidence that the initial ads had, in fact, been paid for in a timely basis. Still, I warned, "We're going to get stuck here. There's no way they can sell enough Korean wigs, and they are going to pay us up to a point and then we'll face a big write-off." My team assured me that wouldn't happen.

One morning a few weeks later I showed up for the meeting and every member of my ad management team—all men, I regret to say now—was wearing a Korean hair wig. Their favorite purveyor of wigs had gone belly-up, and we had seized the warehouse (lawfully, I believe). All we had to show for expending tons of newsprint was thousands of Korean wigs. I don't recall if we ever got any recovery out of that, but somewhere I have a great picture of the ad management of the *San Antonio Light* sheepishly looking like drag queens.

10) "Me Time." It's easy to fall into the trap of thinking the CEO's job is 24/7. It is, but that doesn't mean an all-day, every-day grind. I discovered early what Bruce Springsteen discovered slowly: "Two of the best days of my life were the day I picked up the guitar and the day I learned to put it down." I have to be honest here. Some of my closest associates are a great deal better than I am at "Me Time." But I did learn to use the time away from the office to turn the engines off, recognizing that some of my best thinking came while I was watching sports on TV or pursuing other pleasurable pastimes. For example, I enjoy shooting clay pigeons. Among the useful elements of shooting clay pigeons is learning that you have to shoot where the bird *will be* when the shot gets there, not where the bird *was* when you pulled the trigger; that happens to be true of strategic planning in business. If you can hit them, it's also instant gratification, something we mature adults seldom allow ourselves to experience. I do play golf, which I used to do every weekend but now, regrettably, happens about twenty times a year. When I can't sleep, I review every shot in my last golf game. Counting the shots beats counting sheep for me.

◆

This, above all: When the weeks sail by, dotted with accomplishment, it's useful to appreciate them, but also to remember that they won't all be that way. And when the bottom seems to be dropping out, that, too, won't last. My wife quotes her aunt, who has five children, who always reminded her: "At any time, something is right with at least one." As a CEO, it's your job not to be surprised by that, to be steady and disciplined, to find the right words and the wise response—to justify, in short, your seat at the head of the table.

CHAPTER 9

The Play's the Thing

I n 1979, the banks were not about to lend us the money we needed for acquisitions without a solid base of cash flow. The good news is that we had it—from Hearst Magazines. There were several splendidly edited and managed titles contributing, but just two magazines, *Cosmopolitan* and *Good Housekeeping*, were generating the majority of profits. And to a large extent because of those two magazines, we were able to launch our expansion.

When John Miller turned over the management of the Company to me, magazines accounted for 42 percent of Hearst revenues and more than 60 percent of the earnings generated by all Company operations. By 1982 and 1983, magazines were providing about eight out of every ten dollars of free cash flow the Company's business units were generating—not a staggering amount of money, but with limited backing from banks, it was sufficient to underpin the start of our expansion plans. Gil Maurer gets the lion's share of credit for monetizing those audience-pleasing products, but praise for those successes also rightly belongs to the editors and publishers.

To be precise: praise especially to Helen Gurley Brown and John Mack Carter.

When I tell this story to those who know today's broadly diversified Hearst Corporation, people don't believe it.

It would not be completely accurate to say we could not have created today's Hearst without the success of those two editors, but what was achieved in the first few years of our expansion would have been much slower and more difficult without them.

In 1987, on the occasion of the Company's centennial, we commissioned an illustration depicting the most illustrious executive and creative contributors in our hundred-year history, including the likes of Mark Twain, Jack London, Bob Considine, and Walter Winchell. Yes, those guys all worked for Hearst. But Helen Gurley Brown and John Mack Carter were pictured in the first row.

◆

John Mack Carter is the only editor in the history of American journalism to have edited the "Big Three" women's magazines—*McCall's*, then *Ladies' Home Journal*, and, from 1975 to 1994, *Good Housekeeping*. In his nineteen years at *Good Housekeeping*, as at every magazine along the way, Carter constantly updated his publications.

He achieved the status of a legend when a group of women stormed his office at *Ladies' Home Journal* in 1970 and held him hostage for eleven hours, demanding changes in the magazine. His response was to hear them—and change direction. "There was more discrimination than I thought," he said. "I didn't push our women readers far enough in their self-awareness. . . . Power is the big issue that divides men and women. Men hold power, women

Leave Something on the Table

THE HEARST CENTENNIAL.
100 YEARS OF MAKING
COMMUNICATIONS HISTORY.

Gathered here are a few Hearst employees from the past and present—reporters, columnists, editors, publishers, writers, broadcasters and business executives. Their contributions illustrate the achievements made by thousands of their co-workers over the past century. Together they have made Hearst one of the largest and, we think, one of the best communications companies in the world.

The Hearst Corporation
1887   100 Years of Making Communications History   1987

want power, but men are reluctant to give it—any of it—away." What other male editor would have said this in the early 1970s?

John Mack Carter was instrumental in launching *Victoria*, *Smart Money*, *Marie Claire*, and *Country Living*, which, for a time, was our third most profitable magazine title. One decision he made at *Good Housekeeping* has become standard industry practice in women's magazines: putting celebrities on the cover. The idea was revolutionary at the time, and massive, immediate circulation growth followed.

He had a record of tiring of editing one title and moving on to another. I used to kid him about having edited everything but the "Lower Westchester County Guide to Left-Handed Tennis Players." Keeping John Mack Carter "in place"—that is, making sure he continued to work for Hearst—was among my proudest achievements.

◆

Cosmopolitan was launched in 1886 as a family magazine. It will surprise every reader, I'm sure, to learn that it morphed into a literary magazine. As late as the 1940s, a typical issue might include as many as eight short stories, a short novel, and two serials. *Cosmopolitan* was successful—at its World War II peak, it sold two million copies a month—but the formula became bland over the years, and by 1965 it had lost more than half its readers.

In the 1950s, as she recalled with her typically ruthless honesty, Helen Gurley Brown "had seventeen secretarial jobs, wall to-wall acne, no money, no influential friends, and my IQ was quite average." By 1960, she was an advertising copywriter who bought herself a slightly used Mercedes as a symbol of her success. Then, in 1962, two years after birth control pills became available, she published *Sex and the Single Girl*.

Hearst in 1965 wasn't a company anywhere near the forefront of the women's movement or the sexual revolution. In choosing Helen Gurley Brown as the editor of *Cosmopolitan*, Hearst was throwing the media equivalent of a "Hail Mary" pass. And Helen—who was hired largely on the endorsement of Richard Deems, president of Hearst Magazines at the time—turned out to be a genius choice.

What Helen did was radical, obvious, and simple: She turned the Single Girl into the Cosmo Girl. She wasn't editing for a demographic or a market segment. She created a magazine for a very specific woman: a younger version of herself.

It wasn't coincidental that Helen was married to David Brown, the great movie producer, who earlier in life had been an editor at *Cosmopolitan*. David, often in partnership with Richard Zanuck, produced *Jaws*, *The Sting*, *Driving Miss Daisy*, *The Verdict*, and enough other history-making movies to earn him the coveted Irving G. Thalberg award at the 1990 Oscars. David became my highly valued personal friend and unpaid adviser, along with blessing every contract I ever did with Helen. He was also a master headline writer—he wrote *Cosmo*'s cover lines for Helen, also gratis—and a purveyor of the bold idea, delivered with charm. Some David Brown cover lines will give you the idea. From March 1976: "Change Your Life: Learning How to Assert Yourself Instead of Being Pushed Around." February 1973: "Wives Run Away Too—A Startling Report." And this, also from 1973: "101 Ways a Man Can Please You—If You Would Only Tell Him."

It strikes me that Helen also was a kind of filmmaker—she turned print into scenes in a new world in which those young women could picture themselves. Her personally written newspaper ads around the theme "I guess you could say I'm that Cosmopolitan Girl" perfectly described the cultural movement she created. And month after month, women showed up for the next installment.

In the thirty-two years Helen Gurley Brown was *Cosmo*'s editor—from 1965 to 1997—her work ethic and constantly renewing creativity were a wonder to everyone at Hearst. She labored tirelessly over every word and illustration, turning her magazine into a remarkably profitable business. It's no exaggeration that *Cosmopolitan* was the biggest engine of Hearst's profitability in Helen's first decade there. Over the years, she made *Cosmo* into a cultural phenomenon. There were eventually 64 international editions in 35 languages, and *Cosmo* was distributed in 110 countries—including Mongolia.

◆

Helen and David Brown had luggage and would travel . . . on any free trip, that is. Helen was notoriously cheap. She was known to regularly go back to the table at restaurants and retrieve part of the generous tips David would leave. The Browns did lectures on cruise ships to avoid paying the fare, traveled with the Bennacks and the John Millers to Cairo to raise funds for Madame Jehan Sadat's al Wafa' Wa Amal (Faith and Hope) Rehabilitation Center—I have a great picture of Helen astride a camel—and joined us on a particularly noteworthy trip to San Antonio in 1998. The occasion was a gala honoring Helen for the benefit of the San Antonio Youth Literacy Council. While David was retrieving their luggage at the airport, Helen rushed outside and jumped in a cab. The driver, thinking he was finished for the day, told Helen that he was not available for hire and would she kindly leave his cab. She refused. The police were called, and they actually booked Helen for disturbing the peace, or some such offense. Helen had an unresolved "record" with the San Antonio police for some years, until we pleaded with the authorities to get the charges removed.

During that same visit, Helen came to our ranch in the Hill Country, sixty miles or so west of San Antonio and southwest of Austin. Eagle Bluff Ranch is about 1,800 acres, a representative size by Hill Country standards, but dwarfed by the likes of the King Ranch and numerous other Texas ranches, particularly those in the far western and southern parts of the state. Ours is a working ranch, raising cattle for market. It's also home to several hundred exotic animals from Africa, Asia, and Europe.

At the ranch Helen completed three tasks she had assigned for herself. A triathlon: ride a horse, climb a tree, and skinny-dip. When she learned that Mary Lake Polan and I were getting married, she insisted that Mary Lake also had to complete the triathlon before I would be allowed to marry her. Mary Lake did, declaring the tree climb the most challenging.

The idea that an editor retires at some date—say, after twenty-five years—didn't apply to Helen Gurley Brown. As exceptional as it was when her tenure reached twenty-five years, neither she nor we had any notion that it was time for a change. In 1990, at a glorious party in the Rainbow Room celebrating those twenty-five years, Randolph Hearst and I presented Helen with the keys to a new Mercedes and instructions on how to access her new personal driver. She was thrilled, but it didn't keep her from riding city buses, where she felt she got inspiration from her Cosmo girls.

The understanding we had in the years after that twenty-five-year milestone went something like this: "This isn't going to last forever. If you finish with me before I finish with you, you'll tell me. And that will be it!" I was confident that Helen had endorsed that covenant, although she was always clear that retirement "per se" would not follow her decades in the editor's chair.

Reading the tea leaves and listening carefully to Helen at the end of thirty-one years, I felt that, at age seventy-three, she was ready to agree that we would identify a successor she could train while she remained editor-in-chief. And at some future date she would turn over the reins. Spending her time nurturing the editors of the rapidly growing number of international editions with the title International Editor-in-Chief seemed a next good plan for Helen and for Hearst. She and David had always loved accompanying George Green, the remarkable executive launching new *Cosmopolitans* around the globe, to wherever the next launch was planned.

Gil Maurer had been following the career of Bonnie Fuller, a young but proven editor who had come to the United States to edit *YM* after three years editing *Flare* in her native Canada. With Gil's and my backing, Claeys Bahrenburg, Gil's successor as head of Hearst Magazines, recruited Bonnie to become editor-in-chief of our American version of the successful French title *Marie Claire*. We soon saw her as a possible successor to Helen.

An all-hands-on-deck planning effort began for the day when change would become both good business and agreeable to all. That day came in 1997, Helen's thirty-second year. I was able to recruit Glenda Bailey, the hugely successful editor of the U.K. version of *Marie Claire*, published by a competitive house and progressively diminishing our *Cosmo* readership in Britain, to take the editor's chair at our version of that title. A hat trick, we called it. Glenda to *Marie Claire*, Bonnie to *Cosmopolitan* U.S., and Helen to *Cosmopolitan* International.

This maneuver eventually worked out well, but not without some pain. Helen apparently signaled her best buddies, Liz Smith and Barbara Walters, who were also good friends of mine, that she wasn't quite ready to step down from the mother ship. Several press outlets carried the criticism leveled at us by Liz and Barbara, suggesting that we might be prematurely ending a remarkable publishing career. Worse, according to one of Helen's biographers, Gerri Hirshey, "She told Liz Smith that she was reeling from an article in the *Wall Street Journal*, declaring that she had been axed and outlining the long simmering plans by Hearst to get rid of her."

Helen's feelings were hurt. So were mine. Helen hadn't given me any indication that she wasn't happy, even when I laid out all the details of the transition plan for her. Within reason, her wish had always been my command, and both she and David knew that.

The fallout from that dustup didn't have a long life. Helen knew very well that if the so-called "long simmering plans to get rid of her," as described by the *Journal*, existed at all, they would not have reflected my position, and I was still the boss. Nonetheless, it was a bitter pill for her. She and I talked at great length about the expanded international role, and she rather quickly decided that any extended period of Bonnie Fuller working alongside her wasn't necessary or to her liking. Bonnie was more than ready to take over.

Bonnie Fuller didn't have a long career in the *Cosmo* editor's chair. She gave us a gracefully modernized but still true-to-Helen's-vision *Cosmo*, but after less than two years—too soon for our taste—

she moved on to edit *Glamour* at rival Condé Nast. Once again, we had to answer the question: How do you follow Helen Brown? The answer was already at Hearst: Kate White, then editing *Redbook*.

◆

I learned a lesson from the experience of managing someone as brilliant and motivated as Helen Gurley Brown. She and David became far more than business associates. Our social lives often overlapped. The lesson: There is such a thing as getting too close. It can make carrying out the right business decision harder than it needs to be.

Helen had another decade-long productive and reasonably happy run with our international issues of *Cosmopolitan*, and it was clear that she would never want to retire or to stop coming to the office. Both her health and David's were, by this time, not the best. And then, because she thought of Hearst and me as her family, she pressed me into service to help with the settlement of David's substantial estate after his death in 2010 at the age of ninety-three. I enlisted Eve Burton, Hearst's general counsel, to help. Eve, Mary Lake, Hearst Magazines editorial director Ellen Levine, who had trained under Helen at *Cosmopolitan* and gone on to edit *Woman's Day*, *Redbook*, and *Good Housekeeping*, and Kim St. Clair Bodden, Helen's adoring editorial associate during the Cosmo International period, became a support system. Actually, the family she didn't have. They helped manage everything from Helen's finances to her health care. And Helen wanted me "in the loop" on everything. There was nothing here that would be typical of a CEO's job description, but there was also nothing typical about Helen Gurley Brown.

Helen died in the McKeen Pavilion at New York-Presbyterian Hospital on August 13, 2012, at the age of ninety. One of the most poignant experiences in my professional life was when Eve Burton, Eve's daughter Kat, Kim St. Clair Bodden, Mary Lake, and I flew to Helen's native Arkansas to bury her ashes in Sisco Cemetery, Helen's maternal family cemetery, alongside David's grave and the graves of Helen's mother and sister. Sisco Cemetery is located in Carroll County, Arkansas, the home of the town of Green Forest, where Helen was born and where she had graduated as valedictorian of her high school class.

There was the obligatory funereal rain that day in the Ozarks. Scripture was read, Kat Burton sang "Two Little Girls from Little Rock" from the movie *Gentlemen Prefer Blondes*, and we all had stories to share. New York mayor Michael Bloomberg got this remarkable woman's importance exactly right: "Today New York City lost a pioneer who reshaped not only the entire media industry, but the nation's culture."

Helen had designated Eve Burton and me as trustees of the Helen Gurley Brown Trust. The fruits of Helen's and David's extraordinary achievements are visible at the Brown Institute for Media Innovation at Columbia and Stanford Universities in a remarkable array of charitable and educational causes funded by their estates. Students on both coasts, along with the less fortunate—particularly the young and the elderly—will have better lives far into the future because of their successes.

◆

In a proper history of Hearst, the text would be thick with the names of key players in the drama of an ever-evolving company.

In these pages the focus has been on fewer of my associates and more of our partners. That is the case in part because successful partnerships were the magic sauce most observers believe set the post-1979 Hearst apart from its own history and from everybody else. But Hearst's modern success has been intertwined with magazines, and magazine editors are often quoted and profiled, and let's face it, they're often the most vivid characters in media. So I thought I'd share just a few additional stories here.

After Ellen Levine's basic training at *Cosmopolitan*, we lost her to a rival publishing house, where she took on the role as the top editor of *Woman's Day*. Interestingly we acquired that magazine as part of our Hachette transaction in 2010. When we were able to lure Ellen back to Hearst, her first assignment was *Redbook*. Later she became the first woman in its long history to be editor-in-chief of *Good Housekeeping*. And until recently, she was the first-ever editorial director of Hearst Magazines.

Along with Cathie Black, the extraordinarily persuasive president of Hearst Magazines, Ellen was also instrumental in convincing Oprah Winfrey to join us in the launch of *O, The Oprah Magazine* in 2000. *Adweek* named that magazine Startup of the Year. *Advertising Age* awarded it Best Magazine of the Year and Best Launch of the Year. Those awards were inevitable. *O, The Oprah Magazine* was thought by many seasoned observers to be the most successful start-up ever in the magazine industry. And there were more magazines on the list of successful launches in which Ellen Levine was a major player: the *Food Network Magazine* in 2008, and *HGTV Magazine* in 2012.

Other editors, similar stories. Lou Gropp, who has been editor-in-chief of *House & Garden*, *ELLE DECOR*, and *House Beautiful*, did not come to New York with a deep desire to spend time in exquisite rooms. "I grew up with simple, rather nondescript furniture," he has said. "I didn't dream that people actually worked at these things."

Art-director-turned-editor-in-chief Tony Mazzola breathed much needed life into *Town & Country* and *Harper's BAZAAR*. Of his tenure at *Harper's BAZAAR,* Mazzola said, "We love the handle of being the fashion magazine with a little salt and pepper added." He and his resourceful wife and business partner, Michele, performed an additional uplifting service for Hearst by taking on the role of curator of the fine arts collection in Hearst Tower, a collection largely assembled by Gil Maurer. The collection of artworks on paper guided by Gil's and Tony's shrewd taste in emerging artists means we walk out of our offices into visual refreshment every workday of the year.

Although there doubtlessly are many who would contend that history has recorded other periods when magazines in America boasted higher levels of success and fostered editors-in-chief with greater stature, I would hold out for the years 1980 to 2000. Gil Maurer, Claeys Bahrenburg, Cathie Black, and I were privileged not only to work alongside John Mack Carter, Helen Gurley Brown, Ellen Levine, Lou Gropp, Tony Mazzola, Bonnie Fuller, Kate White, and Glenda Bailey, but also acknowledged masters of their art, like Frank Zachary, Rachel Newman, and Liz Tilberis. Candor and good manners require me to acknowledge that during that same period we competed with many of the all-time best at Condé Nast, Meredith, and elsewhere, including Tina Brown, Grace Mirabella, Anna Wintour, Graydon Carter, Paige Rense, and Myrna Blyth.

The good news is that the editors and creative leaders of our magazines of today are skillfully building their products and their reputations in a world not only of printed magazines on beautiful glossy paper but as digital magazines online. I'm happy to observe a remarkable continuity of quality and values. I'm betting that a new generation of managers, along with a new generation of editors, will perform with an excellence that ratifies the thesis here: Magazines have been, are now, and will far into the future be an essential part of Hearst's greatness as a media company.

CHAPTER 10

The Arc of a Deal

O n January 15, 1979, the acquisition of the *Midland Reporter Telegram* and its sister publication, the *Plainview Daily Herald*, was finalized. Five days later, on January 20, 1979, John Miller handed me the reins to the entire Hearst organization. The debt incurred for the purchase of the stock held by the Foundations had been paid off and we were ready to roll.

From that day in 1979 through 1990, we completed twenty acquisitions and, equally important, launched five new magazine titles and stepped into cable ventures. Five of the acquisitions and three of the magazine start-ups took place in 1979 alone.

I remember fondly that an excited Bill Hearst would stop me in the hall and say, "Frankie, have you been shopping again?"

By 1990 those acquisitions and new launches would account for 42 percent of the earnings being turned in by Hearst operating units. Ten years later, in 2000, those 1979–1990 additions to the Hearst portfolio would represent 67 percent of a Hearst operating profit that had grown fourfold over the decade. The acquisition and new-business-creation programs also continued all through the decade of the 1990s.

Some of those early acquisitions were necessarily modest in size. We had to walk before we could run. Some, however, like the 1986 acquisition of the Boston TV station WCVB-TV and the 1987 purchase of the *Houston Chronicle*, were large by any measure— certainly large for a private company like Hearst. At the time of those transactions the prices we paid for the *Chronicle* and WCVB-TV were said to be the highest ever paid for a single newspaper and a single TV station. Life and media transactions being what they are, both records were later exceeded.

◆

There is an arc to every large acquisition. Those properties that are truly transformational don't just fall in your lap. Relationships play a major role because newspaper and TV station owners care about to whom they are entrusting their hard-won businesses and their valued employees. Then, of course, you have to be ready to pay the highest price.

In 1987, Richard J. V. Johnson, the president of the *Houston Chronicle*, who had tipped me off about the Midland opportunity, called to say that the owner of the newspaper, Houston Endowment, had exhausted every available legal maneuver to avoid the requirement imposed by the Tax Reform Act of 1969—the same act that required the Hearst Foundations to divest the Hearst Corporation common stock. They had no choice: His newspaper would have to be sold. I was immediately interested—I had previously declined an opportunity to acquire the smaller *Houston Post* because I was convinced that the trend to one-newspaper cities would eventually reach Houston, and that the *Chronicle* would almost certainly be the survivor.

I flew to Houston to meet with Johnson and his management team. He told me that he and his senior managers had considered an employee leveraged buyout, a popular trend at the time.

"We can borrow the money," he said. "We just can't pay it back."

Johnson, who was especially well-connected in the industry by virtue of being the chief executive of one of the largest independent newspapers in the country and having been the chairman of ANPA, the American Newspaper Publishers Association, leveled with me: He, the *Chronicle* management, and the leadership at the Houston Endowment liked the idea of a Hearst acquisition. Hearst was a company with a fifty-year history in Texas and had a born-and-bred authentic Texan as its CEO. Still, he made clear that he individually, because of his own industry reputation and personal associations, and the Endowment, for reasons of its fiduciary obligations, would have to shop the transaction. Further, they would have to be satisfied the best price would be paid.

Right then and there I learned the lesson of all lessons about acquisitions: Solid relationships plus the best price will prevail every time.

The late Jesse H. Jones, a prominent Houston mover and shaker, had established Houston Endowment in 1937. Jones had served as head of the Depression-created Reconstruction Finance Corporation and later as secretary of commerce in the Roosevelt administration. Jones and his wife had created Houston Endowment to carry out their personal philanthropy. It was already well-funded, but the *Chronicle* transaction had the prospect to make it the largest private foundation in the state. Its leader in 1987 and the man who carried the title as publisher of the *Chronicle* was

Joseph Howard Creekmore. Although Johnson had influence, he said we would have to persuade Creekmore that Hearst was the best possible buyer.

Creekmore, as the name suggests, had been born on the Creek Indian Reservation in Oklahoma. He was a Native American who moved to Houston to enter Rice Institute, today Rice University, which was a free school in those days. He got his degree in English and history and became a bookkeeper in Jesse Jones's office. Jones ultimately paid his way through Houston Law School. After a highly decorated stint in the Navy in World War II, Creekmore joined Houston Endowment, becoming its president in 1964.

I made thirteen trips to Houston before the *Chronicle* deal was finally sealed. I was studying the details of the business with Johnson, trying to be sure that we could pay back the debt that would be incurred. And I was working to convince Creekmore that we were the ideal buyer. On the second or third trip I asked Gil Maurer to accompany me—nobody had my confidence as to business judgment more than Gil, and this was going to be a long putt.

Gil and I met with Creekmore at his office, which couldn't have been altered much since the Endowment's creation half a century earlier: knotty pine furniture, lithograph pictures on plain wooden walls, rolltop desks. The "offices" were actually divider-partitions with glass at eye level. You had the feeling that it was 1930 all over again. Mr. Creekmore wasn't wearing an eyeshade, but we were almost wondering why not.

It turned out that Howard Creekmore, as he preferred being called, was not only as smart as a treeful of owls, he turned out to be as courageous a stand-up guy as we would ever meet. He held forth at great length about his philosophy of philanthropy, his love of the *Chronicle*, and his disappointment that the Texas representatives in Washington, like George H. W. Bush and Lloyd Bentsen, had not been able to preserve Houston Endowment's continued ownership of the newspaper.

Howard Creekmore reminded us of a straight-back, straight-talking Abe Lincoln. He was from a different era: his was a simpler and more idealistic world than ours. It was completely refreshing to find someone who thought as he did—and in many ways as I do.

After many meetings with Creekmore and the Endowment's lawyers, the discussions and negotiations evolved to the point of Johnson being given a signal by Creekmore: Based on everything—including interactions he and/or Johnson had with Newhouse, Knight Ridder, Warren Buffett, Rupert Murdoch, and others—Hearst would be the right buyer and the price would have to be $400 million. Gil and I were set back on our heels. This was as much as we had paid the year earlier for Boston television station WCVB-TV, and that station had earnings vastly above anything the *Chronicle* had ever achieved.

There followed one of the most important and memorable episodes on the road to building the new Hearst. After half a dozen trips during which we watched our expenses, I decided we should pamper ourselves and live like executives being asked to spend $400 million on a newspaper—we moved to the exclusive Post Oak, reputed to be among the best hotels in town, and decided to take a long, clarifying walk.

Was there any chance we could make this deal pay off? Was it really that important that Hearst's newspaper division be returned to national prominence? After all, we were doing great in the magazine division, and we had made solid deals in buying the Boston, Kansas City, and Dayton TV stations. The *Chronicle* was profitable but not resoundingly so, and in fact Johnson and his key associates had almost passed out when we showed them how much we would expect the *Chronicle* to earn to justify the price that was being asked.

But we were young and committed to elevating our company on its one-hundredth birthday. Gil and I agreed: Look how much progress we'd made in the seven or eight years we'd been in charge. I had talked to enough of our directors that I felt confident we had the necessary backing. Let's do it!

So we told Creekmore and Johnson that we had a deal at $400 million. We did ask for one concession: We'd like to pay $300 million in cash, and to give the Endowment our note for $100 million, and we'd like an attractive interest rate.

I'll always remember that Creekmore said he would rather have a piece of Hearst "paper"—our IOU—than a U.S. Government bond. We were home free.

◆

Or so we thought.

On March 13, 1987, the front page of the *Houston Chronicle* ran a bold headline announcing that the paper had been sold for $400 million to the Hearst Corporation. A rather flattering picture of Howard Creekmore, Richard J. V. Johnson, and me, ostensibly signing the contracts, occupied more of page one than is typical.

But, stunningly, a signed contract did not mean a sale.

State Attorney General Jim Mattox, like all attorneys general, had jurisdiction over charitable organizations in the state—and here was a great opportunity to flex his muscles. Mattox, who had served in the U.S. House of Representatives for three terms, had been elected attorney general in 1983. That same year he had also been indicted for "commercial bribery" and had been acquitted. He narrowly won reelection in 1986. The win was narrow because of public outrage over his allegedly having threatened the influential law firm of Fulbright & Jaworski with the loss of its tax-exempt bond practice, another power held by the attorney general of Texas. The threat was the result of the law firm's representation of Mobil Oil Co., during which it sought to depose Mattox's sister, Janice, in connection with campaign money entanglements. (Leon Jaworski, the firm's named partner, the reader will recall, had served as the special prosecutor in Watergate following the firing of Archibald Cox.)

The Associated Press noted in the story about his death in 2008 that Mattox "fought efforts to spare condemned inmates from death. He routinely traveled to Huntsville to attend executions in Texas."

In short, Mr. Mattox prided himself on being the toughest guy in the crowd—in any crowd. And now he had a chance to show some New Yorkers just how tough. He had become aware, apparently through discovery of letters dated October 27, 1986, and March 10, 1987, that another publisher with clearly limited financial capacity had proposed purchase prices of $500 million and $415 million, respectively. The intruding publisher claimed he hadn't been given an adequate opportunity to bid. Mattox contacted Creekmore and directed him not to finalize our transaction.

What now? Neither we nor Houston Endowment believed the offer was real.

Creekmore stood up. On April 2, 1987, he wrote Mattox a detailed history of how the Endowment had shopped the paper to responsible and financially able newspaper publishers and how the Hearst transaction was the best he could do. Creekmore made it clear he had no intention of pursuing the deal advanced by the other publisher, because, he wrote, "information available to me indicated very clearly that he did not have the means to accomplish a purchase of the Chronicle, and his offer appeared to be unrealistically high."

Creekmore attached a fairness opinion letter written by Morton Newspaper Research. He also provided copies of nondisclosure agreements to access *Chronicle* financial information signed by executives at the *New York Times*, Knight Ridder, and A. H. Belo, owner of the *Dallas Morning News*, and, not so incidentally, me.

Creekmore also referenced a Dun & Bradstreet credit report indicating the interfering publishing company had a net worth of "approximately $35,000,000."

Mattox did not yield.

For what must have been the eleventh or twelfth trip to Houston, Gil and I chartered a Lockheed JetStar, a 1960s corporate jet jocularly known for having as many engines (four) as it carried passengers—although that was apocryphal—and we flew to Houston. After comparing notes with the *Chronicle* folks and Creekmore, we contacted the attorney general's office and asked for a meeting. Mattox agreed to meet us at the Headliners Club, a popular Austin watering hole frequented by press types, used-to-be press types, and distinguished locals.

LEFT: Future Hearst CEO Frank and mother Louisiana "Lula" Wardell (Connally) Bennack, circa 1935. RIGHT: Frank's dad, Frank Sr. (left), in theatrical mode with the cast of a San Antonio adaptation of the Broadway play *A Slight Case of Murder*, 1936.

LEFT: Frank, hair combed and ready to go to work, at age eight, circa 1941. TOP RIGHT: On the set of *Time for Teens* at KEYL: Frank and contestants for Teen Queen, circa 1950. BOTTOM RIGHT: Program Director Bill Robb (left) and Frank enjoy reading the *Time for Teens* fan mail pouring into the studio, 1950.

In his newly gained publisher's office, Frank holds his beloved *San Antonio Light*, circa 1968.

International construction company leader H.B. Zachry, Frank Massi, Richard Berlin, and George Hearst Sr. with Frank at the grand opening of the *San Antonio Light* pressroom, circa 1970.

LEFT: Colonel B. J. Horner, Frank's predecessor as publisher of *San Antonio Light*, chats with Mayor Walter W. McAllister, Fort Sam Houston, circa 1965. RIGHT: Frank after a "winning" shot against Bobby Riggs, who is dressed in his muumuu and carries a valise, San Antonio, 1973.

Three sons of William Randolph Hearst with Frank (center) and Frank's predecessor John R. Miller (right) in 1979. From left: David Whitmire Hearst, Randolph A. Hearst, and William Randolph Hearst Jr.

Democratic presidential nominee Jimmy Carter with Frank at Hearst during the Democratic National Convention, 1976.

LEFT: President Ronald Reagan and Frank at the White House during a meeting with Hearst newspaper editors, circa 1981. RIGHT: W. R. Hearst Jr., Major General Charles Sweeney, and Frank lay wreaths at the Hearst-funded Eagle Squadrons Memorial in London, 1986.

LEFT: Witness to history at an Associated Press luncheon, Frank looks on as former President Richard Nixon has what was believed to be his first encounter with *Washington Post* publisher Katharine Graham since *Post* reporting was credited with exposing much of the Watergate scandal, 1985. RIGHT: *Houston Chronicle* President Richard J. V. Johnson and Frank at the press conference announcing the Hearst acquisition, 1987.

British Prime Minister Margaret Thatcher with Frank at the celebration of Hearst UK's 75th anniversary, 1985.

Luella Bennack (center) and the Bennack girls with Frank, circa 1987. Standing, from left: Julie, Laura, and Shelley. Seated: Diane and Cindi.

Liza Minnelli celebrates with Frank following her performance at Hearst's 100th anniversary gala, Waldorf Astoria, 1987.

Former First Lady Nancy and President Ronald Reagan joined by (from left) Leonard Goldenson, Bob Hope, Jack Hausman, and Frank at the Waldorf Astoria, circa 1990.

LEFT: A confident Vice President George H. W. Bush and Frank immediately prior to Bush's election as president in 1988. RIGHT: Hearst-Argyle Television executives ring the opening bell at the New York Stock Exchange in 1998.

Chairman of the Board George R. Hearst Jr. (left) and Director and former Chief Operating Officer Gil Maurer with Frank at Hearst, circa 2000.

LEFT: Helen Gurley Brown deep in conversation with Frank, circa 2000. RIGHT: Former Editor-in-Chief of *Good Housekeeping* John Mack Carter with Frank, circa 2000.

Oprah Winfrey with Frank celebrating the remarkable success of *O, The Oprah Magazine*, 2001.

Gil Maurer, Vice President and General Counsel Eve Burton, and former Chief Financial Officer Ronald Doerfler with Frank in hard hats during construction of Hearst Tower, circa 2004.

Architect Norman Foster joins Frank and real estate developer Jerry Speyer in hoisting a beam at Hearst Tower, circa 2005.

Gil Maurer and recently appointed President and CEO Steve Swartz join Frank on the fifty-six-foot escalator at Hearst Tower, 2013. Photographed by Jonathan Becker for *Fortune*.

LEFT: Former President Bill Clinton and Frank at the dedication of the Vivian and Seymour Milstein Family Heart Center at NewYork-Presbyterian/Columbia University Medical Center, 2006. RIGHT: Julie Andrews with Frank at The Paley Center for Media, 2009.

LEFT: Jazz legend Wynton Marsalis (center) and Lincoln Center President Reynold Levy with Frank at Lincoln Center, circa 2010. RIGHT: Mary Lake Polan with husband Frank at the 2011 Paley Honors, commemorating his twenty years as chairman of The Paley Center for Media.

Barbara Walters with Frank at The Paley Center for Media gala at the Waldorf Astoria, 2001.

LEFT: Hearst's soon-to-be CEO Steve Swartz and Publisher and CEO of the Albany *Times Union* George Hearst III with Frank at an onsite press dedication, 2013. RIGHT: In 2013, former President Carter and Frank reprise Carter's 1976 visit to Hearst.

CLOCKWISE FROM TOP LEFT: Mayor Michael Bloomberg and The Paley Center for Media President and CEO Pat Mitchell with Frank, 2011. Ralph Lauren and Frank embrace, 2013. Frank and Jennifer Hudson celebrate Hearst's 125th anniversary in 2012. Mary Lake and Frank showing off at a Hearst offsite meeting, 2012.

LEFT: Disney Chairman and CEO Robert A. Iger with Frank at a Lincoln Center event honoring Iger, 2008. RIGHT: "Long Gray Line," a homecoming of past Hearst executives and creative leaders assembled by Frank, 2013.

TOP LEFT: Former Secretary of State Henry Kissinger and Frank at The Paley Center for Media, 2015. BOTTOM LEFT: President Barack Obama with Frank at the Gridiron Club Dinner, 2013. RIGHT: Barbra Streisand with Frank following her Master Class at Hearst Tower, 2014.

Historian Doris Kearns Goodwin being interviewed by Frank at a Hearst offsite meeting at Eagle Bluff Ranch, 2016.

Steve Swartz presents Frank with the trophy signifying his 2017 induction into the Advertising Hall of Fame.

LEFT: Portrait by artist Margaret Holland Sargent that was hung in 2013 to commemorate Frank's twenty-eight years as CEO of Hearst. TOP RIGHT: Illustration of a Bennack-ism by Tom Armstrong, creator of the comic strip *Marvin*. BOTTOM RIGHT: Hearst Board Chairman William R. Hearst III (right) and Frank with Senate Youth Program students in Washington, D.C., circa 2014.

We made the case that our offer was a full one and that nobody was likely to pay more, or for that matter as much. Mattox said that we needed to make some concession—or he would continue to block the deal.

Gil and I took a break to caucus while, presumably, Mattox had another drink. We decided we'd agree to pay $410 million, an extra $10 million, even though we thought we were being had. We put that on the table. Mattox countered that he would let the deal go forward if we would increase the offer to $415 million, and increase the interest rate we had agreed to pay on the note the Endowment would hold from 5 percent to 7 percent. Our view was that Mattox was exercising his power in an abusive manner simply because he could.

In a second caucus Gil and I reasoned—or, more accurately, rationalized—that this roughly 4 percent increase in the purchase price wouldn't determine whether we had made a good deal or not. And we soothed our feelings by remembering that the money was not going into anybody's pocket but to an endowment that funded education and numerous worthy causes.

We said okay, and on April 30, 1987, Mattox wrote to me at the Endowment's address, and not only articulated that the deal was now fair and could proceed, but wished Hearst "success in this expansion of its investment in our state."

Happily, the *Chronicle* would prove to be an excellent investment, paying for itself several times over.

CHAPTER 11

Proving the Thesis: Relationships and the Highest Price Win Every Time

When a company is in acquisition mode, what's needed for success is a strong balance sheet, an adequate line of credit, and close contact with investment bankers. Right?

Not wrong, but also not the best scenario either. Sure, today most sales of companies end up being handled in auctions led by investment bankers, but efforts by a CEO to build relationships with the owners of potential target companies can still pay a dividend. The relationship component is particularly valuable when the acquiring company seeks a specific business or a clearly identified asset to round out its holdings or strengthen its competitive position.

This approach contrasts with randomly evaluating whatever comes to market through the investment banker process. Make no mistake, investment bankers can and do play a valuable role as advisers and in helping to manage both the process of divestiture and acquisition. Investment bankers brought some of our most successful acquisitions to us. But in my view the pendulum has swung further from the principal-to-principal process than is ideal.

It appears to me now in hindsight that our most concentrated and successful period of acquisition benefited significantly from deals being done between principals.

One of my favorite memories relates to the process leading to our purchase in 1986 of television station WCVB-TV in Boston.

Shortly after I became Hearst CEO, probably in 1979 or 1980, a senior colleague, Richard E. Deems, suggested that if I was serious about pivoting the Company to an electronic future I should meet an old friend of his. That friend was John Kluge, founder of Metromedia, Inc., at the time the largest independent television entity in the United States. Deems, a major figure in Hearst as early as the 1940s as president of Hearst Magazines, and then serving as an influential board member and Family trustee, had an apartment in the Waldorf Towers. So, too, did Kluge.

That introduction spawned a warm friendship that played out in both Kluge's and my pro bono and business lives over the next two decades.

John Werner Kluge was born in 1914 in Chemnitz, Germany. He immigrated to the United States in 1922. He earned a scholarship to Columbia University and got an economics degree there in 1937. Over the years he built a television empire around independent stations, which is to say stations not affiliated with one of the three television networks. Metromedia also owned two network-affiliated stations, in Kansas City and Minneapolis.

Those two network-affiliated stations caught my attention. Owning them seemed inconsistent with Metromedia's strategy of dominating the lucrative independent niche in metropolitan cities, as the name implied. As we would see each other socially or in connection with our pro bono interests, including United Cerebral Palsy, I made it clear that if Kluge were ever a seller of those network affiliates we would be an aggressive buyer. Those stations would fit our strategy perfectly.

My persistence paid off. Early in 1982 Kluge called to say that he was planning to bid on a Boston station. Because regulation at the time permitted ownership of only seven stations, he would have to divest one station. We could buy station KMBC in Kansas City . . . if we were ready to do a deal he had in mind. Always being extraordinarily skilled in tax avoidance, Kluge envisioned a transaction that would avoid his having to pay any tax on the appreciated value of the Kansas City station. We would acquire the Boston station, WCVB-TV, and then in a like-for-like trade, sell him Boston, in return for which we would receive the Kansas City station and a cash amount sufficient to make up the sizable difference in the value of the two stations. Our lawyers blessed the transaction as perfectly legal, routine, and consistent with applicable tax rules. We agreed on price and shook hands on the deal.

After the usual wait for regulatory approval of the transaction, we gathered at the offices of Kluge's attorney to finalize the transaction. Boston station WCVB-TV was signed over to Hearst. Before I signed the papers that would transfer the station over to Metromedia, I stopped the proceedings and said something akin to the following to Kluge: "John, we're excited about owning Kansas City. I'm grateful that you came to me. Like you, we're anxious to grow. My broadcast guys are familiar with the sterling performance record of WCVB-TV in Boston. Before I sign this, can I get you to promise that if you ever sell Boston you will come to us?"

Kluge's head was moving up and down, giving me a clear "yes" answer even before I had finished with the request. I continued, "I seriously doubt that will ever happen, John, but thanks for the commitment."

Handshake, joint signatures.

Kluge and I saw each other frequently in the months after that. The Bennacks were almost always included in any major social gathering the Kluges would host, including several glamorous weekend parties at his fabulous Charlottesville estate and on his personal yacht. The guests often talked about John's desire to share the good life he had earned with friends and business associates. The events often connected to his growing philanthropy. He liked to stage events around his birthdays, at which in his remarkably understated voice he would announce a major gift to a medical or educational institution, then turn the evening over to performances by his pals Tony Bennett, k.d. lang, or Vic Damone.

A word about that voice. I always believed that Kluge had a carefully planned, well-practiced style of speaking so softly that listeners would have to strain to hear him. The style was particularly effective when Kluge was speaking to a group. There was absolute quiet as everyone in the room would lean forward and listen intently to every word.

Late in 1985, a little more than three years after our Kansas City/Boston transaction, John Kluge called with the news that he had decided to sell the Boston station. He asked if we were still interested. I assured him we were. I asked the price. "A mere $450 million," says he.

Gulp.

It was true that multiples of cash flow being paid for stations had risen in the three years since Kluge's purchase of WCVB. In 1984 the Federal Communications Commission had relaxed the rule of seven stations maximum and allowed a single owner to own twelve stations. That alone had contributed to higher prices, as previously foreclosed television owners entered the market to expand their holdings. And the Massachusetts Miracle of the 1980s was real—the Boston market was on an economic roll, resulting in higher earnings at the station. Perhaps most importantly, WCVB was among the largest, if not the single largest, network-affiliated stations not owned by one of the networks. This was an opportunity not likely to come to market again anytime soon.

I told my friend Kluge that we'd find a way to get there on price. He raised two other potential obstacles. Given the earlier history of local ownership of the station, Kluge said that the senior management at the station had been rumored to be interested in a leveraged buyout and would have some chance of raising the money from local businessmen. He thought such a transaction would be more difficult for Metromedia, and, more importantly, a promise is a promise. He wanted to deliver on the pledge he had made to me three years ago. The prospect of the sale would have to be kept quiet and we would need to get the local management on board once a sale to us was announced.

One more thing: John Kerry, elected that year as senator from Massachusetts, had indicated he would be very interested in who the buyer was if the station were sold. Transfer of a broadcast license is not something that technically requires approval of local or federal officeholders, but the FCC would certainly give weight to any opposition raised by such a powerful force as a U.S. senator.

Bostonians were proud and proprietary about this great television station. More than one knowledgeable commentator had described WCVB-TV as the nation's best. How could we keep the matter secret while we worked through details of the transaction? We would need to make a site visit, evaluate the state of the station's technology along with extensive review of the financial and operating records.

Kluge arranged a "midnight raid," as we called it. A small group of my associates and I could visit the station late at night, after the staff, or most of them, had gone home. Robert "Bob" Bennett, the truly inspirational entrepreneur, shareholder, and CEO of the station—and the driving force in the station's excellence—agreed to meet us and show us around.

I pulled together a small "invasion force"—Gil Maurer, John Conomikes, our general manager of broadcasting, and one or two others—and we flew to Boston late one night. We were met at the airport by an effusive limo driver who had been sworn to secrecy, presumably by Bennett. He delivered us to the station's side entrance that night, and from that moment on he was a fixture in our lives, always believing he had been a co-conspirator in our successful purchase of the station. He met me and my associates on every future trip to the station.

Sotto voce Bennett met us at the service entrance and we exchanged pleasantries. The "midnight raid" ensued. We quietly walked through every corner of the station: newsroom, studios, control rooms, advertising and business offices. Bennett answered our questions and described, with justified pride, why this was no ordinary television station.

Only the cleaning people were encountered as we moved about.

At some point we heard a loud voice inquiring: "Hey, Bob, are those the new owners?" I don't recall whether Bennett responded, but I'm sure he didn't acknowledge our purpose or even say who we were.

We learned that the handsome gentleman blowing our cover was Chet Curtis; he and his wife, Natalie Jacobson, were the station's and Boston's most beloved news anchor team. Curtis had hung around after the late newscast to work on a story for the next day.

At a subsequent luncheon with Kluge I learned that, true to his tax avoidance inclinations, he had placed the buildings that housed all his stations, including Boston, into some kind of tax-advantaged real estate trust and that Hearst wouldn't be able to own the building for several years. During what he would always refer to as "my $10 million luncheon," I got Kluge to reduce the purchase price, recognizing we would have to buy the building later separately, which we did.

The time came for a public announcement. Almost all of the details had been worked out. We hadn't met with Senator Kerry or the senior station staff, but those meetings could hardly be held as long as the transaction was not publicly known. We had to have faith we could navigate the issues related to those elements. Kluge arranged for us to meet in New York at the Waldorf Towers one morning with the understanding we'd sign the papers, meet the station manager, Jim Coppersmith, and the public announcement would follow.

As we entered the Towers lobby, I was somewhat taken aback at the sight of Rupert Murdoch and Barry Diller, both of whom I knew but neither of whom I understood had anything to do with our transaction. It didn't take long for us to learn that they hadn't expected to see us there either, and that Kluge skillfully and secretly had entered into deals to sell us Boston and to sell Murdoch, technically 20th Century Fox Film Corp., all the other Metromedia stations.

Despite the importance of our transaction, we were a sidecar of sorts to the founding of the Fox network, of which the Metromedia independent stations would be the foundation. Our $450 million purchase of WCVB would be judged to be the highest price paid for a single television station at that time. But it wouldn't be big news alongside a $2 billion purchase of the remaining seven Metromedia stations by an international media mogul with great success in his native Australia and in the U.K., now transitioning into American citizenship and prospectively directing his focus to shaking up the U.S. television network landscape.

Jim Coppersmith had a cogent way of describing the proceedings that followed: "Everybody else turned left into a room with Murdoch and Diller, and I turned right into the hands of Frank Bennack and Hearst."

By the time we met with Senator Kerry, he had been well-briefed on who we were and the nature of the media properties we owned and operated and was clearly comfortable to welcome us to Boston.

More interesting was the way we dealt with one of the nation's most skilled and experienced senior television staffs, the men and women who made the Boston station preeminent. We concluded what they cared about most was the preservation of the high quality that had characterized the operations at channel 5, WCVB-TV. To win them over we needed to show them that Hearst media properties, in print and on the screen, had the same devotion to quality and public service as did their general manager, news director, chief engineer, program director, public affairs director, local and national sales managers, and their senior associates, who all had the same pride as if they had been owners.

We decided to pull together a delegation of our top editors and creative leaders from magazines, broadcasting, newspapers, book publishing, and feature syndication, and have our Boston colleagues-to-be fly down to our New York headquarters for a show-and-tell luncheon in the *Good Housekeeping* dining room: "Here's what matters to us: How about you?" I think we all left that day as one family devoted to the proposition that what really mattered was what we put on the page and on the screen. I remember Helen Gurley Brown saying to me after that session that she never felt better about the talent we were assembling under the Hearst umbrella.

How did doing business with John Kluge work out in the long run? KMBC-TV in Kansas City and WCVB-TV in Boston have, together and separately, handsomely returned the full investment Hearst made in them, including the interest expense we apply in analyzing acquisitions whether or not we used borrowed money for the transaction. Equally important, both stations are high-performing components of a television group that continues to be a major contributor to Hearst's bottom line.

◆

Often the relationships that get built before and during a transaction last long after a deal is finalized. John Kluge and I didn't do any more business after that day at the Waldorf Towers but we remained warm and supportive friends. He would personally call to ensure that I was available on the date he planned for his birthday parties, a practice that continued right up until the day in 2010 he called to be sure that Mary Lake and I could attend his ninety-sixth birthday party. He passed away a few days after the phone call. His wife, Maria Tussi Kuttner Kluge, and the Kluge family decided to go ahead with the party and turn it into a combination funeral, birthday celebration, and memorial tribute to this remarkable man's life. What a great idea and what a memorable event!

That day started at the Kluges' Charlottesville farm. The five hundred or so guests moved to Monticello Memorial Gardens for the funeral. After inspiring speeches with an appropriate religious message, we passed by the casket, sprinkling rose petals and handfuls of earth into the open grave. The music in the background, Leonard Cohen's "Hallelujah," seemed perfect for the occasion.

Then we celebrated John's birthday at the party he had planned. It could not have been more festive. Tussi had requested that a few of us give brief remarks about our lives with John. I shared the favorite story he had told me about a youthful college student named John Kluge:

"Frank, I was paying my living expenses getting through Columbia, where I had a scholarship, by playing poker. At one point, the faculty member supervising me warned that if I continued to play poker on campus, I would risk losing my scholarship. I told him they would never catch me playing poker again."

John would pause and smile, letting you know he meant they wouldn't *catch* him, not that he would stop playing.

He would continue: "One night I had the gang over for the usual game, and I got dealt three 5s in a five card stud game. No sooner had I realized I probably had a winner when there was a knock on the door. The authorities had caught up with us! As we scrambled to get out of there, poker chips went flying in one direction, cards in another, money in another."

Another Kluge pause. "You know, Frank, I never got three 5s again until I got Channel 5 in New York, Channel 5 in Washington, and Channel 5 in Boston."

CHAPTER 12

It's Not Who You Know. It's How You Know Them. And How They Know You.

I was beyond busy in my first days as CEO of Hearst, but because I believed that I should broaden my contacts and knowledge by getting involved with other institutions and causes, I joined several public company boards, never more than two at a time. Early on I joined the boards of Allied Stores and Manufacturers Hanover Trust, a predecessor bank to today's J.P. Morgan. Later, American Home Products (later known as Wyeth Pharmaceutical Company) and—possibly the most popular with my family—the Ralph Lauren Corporation asked me to join their boards.

Leonard Goldenson, the head of ABC, and I served on the board of Allied Stores together. Our early childhoods were congruent: towns distant from New York, strong work ethics inherited from our parents, high school sports, an interest in show business. From there, our paths diverged—dramatically. He was admitted to Harvard at sixteen without taking an exam, swiftly climbed the ranks at Paramount Pictures, and after orchestrating a merger, became head of ABC, where, among numerous innovations, he oversaw the introduction of the *Movie of the Week*, *Wide World of*

Sports, and other pathfinding programs that led his network from last to first in the ratings.

Leonard was everything I thought a CEO should be. He took cabs to meetings and flew economy class; in short order, other executives did. He created a media empire noted for its civility. And he was civic-minded. One of his children was born with cerebral palsy. In 1949, he and his wife, Isabelle, were founders of United Cerebral Palsy, among the first charities to raise money with telethons.

Leonard initially befriended me because Hearst was an ABC affiliate, although a minor one, and because I had followed in the footsteps of my predecessors as a supporter of United Cerebral Palsy, a cause of extraordinary importance to him. But I think it was our shared values that led us to become friends.

One afternoon, before the start of an Allied board meeting, Leonard and I talked about a new phenomenon: cable networks. At that time, cable was still primarily a technology to help deliver a better signal in cities where there wasn't a direct line of sight from the tower to the home. Both Leonard and I believed that a relatively new and still small trend to deliver original content via cable would make the business more meaningful. He had placed a modest bet on a prospective channel to be called "Arts" and planned to create a showplace for the performing arts at a higher level than previously available on home screens. Perhaps, with a smaller audience on cable, that programming would succeed.

Leonard agreed that Hearst's expertise in women's issues through our women's magazines might also lead to interesting cable programming. Broadcasting? Hearst? When I took over from John Miller we had three TV stations, each of which was affiliated with one of the three networks. Later, we added two more. We were still well under scale.

I had heard somebody say, "The broadcasting business is a bit like Wagner's music—better than it sounds." With my TV history, I believed it. And I thought that the skills and experience of ABC and Hearst together might just produce something promising. Notice the "might." As Leonard and I agreed, "Everybody is going to lose a lot of money in this business before it pays off. Why don't we jump into it together?"

From that conversation, we decided to form a joint venture, Hearst-ABC Video Services. The decision for Hearst to be the first name in that enterprise was made with a coin toss—on a phone call between Leonard's associate Herb Granath and my cable colleague Ray Joslin.

We had seven years of losses on the original iterations of what became A&E and Lifetime. For a company like ours—and for that matter, a company like Goldenson's ABC in those days—seven years of losses was something to be concerned about. Some board members were saying, "Where is this going? Seven years is a very long time."

Those were the best losses Hearst ever endured. We built good businesses at Lifetime and A&E. Then The History Channel, our very successful A&E spinoff championed by A&E CEO Nick Davatzes, who was largely responsible for the success enjoyed by both networks. His successors—Abbe Raven, Nancy Dubuc, and Paul Buccieri—ably built on that achievement.

Those successes mattered in the short run; they mattered more later. We never would have gotten the opportunity to own a portion of ESPN had we not gone into business with ABC.

◆

ESPN was the brainchild of Bill Rasmussen, who wanted to broadcast University of Connecticut basketball games to the entire state. Then he learned that a satellite transponder could carry sports to the entire country. That was more ambitious than he'd planned, but he plunged into it. On September 7, 1979—nine months after I became CEO of Hearst—ESPN began broadcasting.

Leonard Goldenson had invested in a minority interest in ESPN and, stimulated by his associates Fred Pierce and Herb Granath, acquired in 1984 the interest ABC didn't already own. The price: $188 million. Because it was a small side business for ABC, Goldenson started thinking about partners. As we were ABC's partners in other cable networks, ABC considered asking us.

Instead, ABC made the deal with Nabisco.

Why? Two reasons. Ross Johnson, Nabisco's CEO, had fat ad budgets that could surely help the fledgling sports network. And Johnson liked to hang around with athletes.

Somewhat to my surprise, on March 19, 1985, Goldenson called to tell me that he was selling ABC to Capital Cities, a splendid operator of television stations and newspapers led by Thomas S. Murphy and Daniel Burke. Cap Cities would now be our partner in the cable joint ventures and our ABC-affiliated television stations. Given our personal relationship and business success, I never would have wished for a change from Leonard Goldenson, but I knew and highly respected both Murphy and Burke and had no doubt they would be good partners. Great partners turned out to be a more accurate appraisal. Cap Cities became the owners of the majority of ESPN when the ABC deal closed in 1986.

In time, the R.J. Reynolds Tobacco Company (RJR) acquired Nabisco. Then Kohlberg Kravis Roberts (KKR) acquired RJR Nabisco in one of the most talked about and written about transactions in modern business history, as detailed in the bestselling book *Barbarians at the Gate*. The price of RJR Nabisco was large, to say the least, and so was the debt—it made sense to sell assets that didn't serve the core business. ESPN wasn't key to tobacco or food.

As required, RJR consulted Cap Cities/ABC, which maintained approval rights on any sale of the 20 percent stake.

Dan Burke, who had succeeded Tom Murphy as Cap Cities/ABC CEO, called me.

"A piece of ESPN is available," he said. "What do you think?"

◆

A piece of ESPN?

Gil Maurer, now COO, and I looked at each other and had the same thought: Audiences of men are hard to aggregate, but they crave sports, especially live sports. The possibilities for programming, advertising, and sponsorship were obvious, although the level of success ESPN had achieved against those possibilities by that time was still quite modest or Cap Cities/ABC would have gobbled up the 20 percent it didn't own. Gil and I thought it was very, very likely that there was substantial upside potential at ESPN. We decided this was a deal we had to do.

KKR's newly acquired unit wanted more for the asset than I thought appropriate, but after KKR tested the market, Cap Cities signaled to us that a deal might get done at what we might consider a more rational price.

Some influential forces at Hearst questioned the investment. Their general opinion: "It's only 20 percent. ESPN's got a bunch of stuff that I don't care to watch. Why are you wanting to do this?"

Well, I'm a sports fan. I was a sports participant in my youth, as was Gil Maurer, and I know how valuable sports rights can be. Nobody knew that ESPN would become the business that it is today. I was no different, but I knew it was going to make more money than we paid for it, and that's a pretty good way to think about acquisitions.

The most vivid knock on ESPN was, as we kept hearing, that it was "a channel that mainly broadcasts stuff like tractor pulls." That turned out to be a good reason to make the investment. ESPN didn't have much of a programming lineup yet, which was the obvious reason for the price we were able to negotiate.

Because stock market analysts have suggested ESPN is now worth $30 billion or substantially more, Hearst's ability to buy 20 percent of the company for $167 million is sometimes called "the deal of the century," though that might just be a bit of an exaggeration.

This is not an exaggeration: Our pivot to cable networking was the single largest triumph in Hearst's modern history. And the most significant: Our cable partnership—Lifetime, A&E, and The History Channel—and the investment in ESPN have been more responsible for where the company is today financially than any other acquisition or launch in the company's history, although happily we were able to pick a few more winners. And now the company's recent acquisitions are leading to even greater diversification.

I'm sometimes asked: Dan Burke could have called anyone—why did he call you?

Set aside that Hearst is a private company, and we could respond to the offer quickly. Set aside that we had established a record for paying a fair price instead of embarking on a grinding negotiation. Set aside that Burke and Murphy knew we were interested in expanding and diversifying, and that, unlike many companies, we were enthusiastic partners and good at it.

Focus, instead, on the human factor—on personal relationships. Because of personal relationships, Cap Cities had been able to acquire ABC. And because Murphy and Burke knew me and Hearst from our cable joint ventures and from our industry and the pro bono activities we shared, they thought we spoke a common language and had common values. And they adopted Leonard Goldenson's view that Hearst and I had proved to be good partners.

◆

You can't know how well a relationship works until it's tested.

In 1996, Cap Cities/ABC was sold to The Walt Disney Company for $19 billion, the third largest amount in a merger transaction up until that time. We had yet another partner. Sometime later, when the renewals of the NFL contracts came up for the networks, our partners at Disney weren't sure they could afford the rights cost required for ESPN to air a full season of Sunday night games and for the ABC network to continue its fabled *Monday Night Football* broadcasts.

Disney CEO Michael Eisner called to tell me that Disney simply didn't think it could pay what it was going to take to get the NFL renewed for ABC. ESPN's a different matter, he said. Eisner thought a possible solution would be to allocate more of the combined cost to ESPN, but that would have the effect of significantly increasing Hearst's share, since we were bearing 20 percent of the ESPN expense. He didn't think he could expect us to do that.

Well, we offered to do exactly that. We ultimately paid millions more than our share. Michael was grateful. Yes, it turned out to be in our interest—football was a key ingredient in the strength and growth of ESPN. But I don't think Eisner was completely surprised. There was a reason for Hearst to bear a greater share of the expense, and we both knew it—it was good partnership conduct. Given how valuable acquiring our piece of ESPN had turned out to be, we couldn't possibly act as if we had no reason to step up and help Disney.

If the situation were reversed, would Eisner or his successor, Bob Iger, have volunteered to help Hearst?

I'd bet on it.

CHAPTER 13

We Had Plans for an Office Tower. Despite 9/11, We Built It.

Although the Hearst Corporation had its origins in California, it has had a presence in New York City for all but eight of its 132-year existence. I have been associated with the Company for sixty-eight years—half of its history—and I have been present in the New York headquarters for forty-five years. I can say without fear of contradiction that nothing during my time in New York has more identified Hearst with this greatest of cities than Lord Foster's iconic Hearst Tower, authorized in 2001 in the immediate aftermath of 9/11 and opened in 2006.

William Randolph Hearst never started anything he couldn't make bigger, and the Hearst Building at 959 Eighth Avenue (now 300 West 57th Street) was no exception. The founder envisioned a media center on that site, and the building that Joseph Urban created for Hearst's twelve magazines in 1928 signaled his grand ambition. Just consider the large themes of the statues set on the rim of the face: Comedy, Tragedy, Music, Art, Industry, Printing, and Science.

If Mr. Hearst had titanic ambitions for his magazine company, why wasn't its headquarters bigger? For one thing, the budget of

$2 million was far from a bargain for a six-story building. For another, that cost—$28.5 million in today's dollars—was dwarfed by a far grander project Hearst was self-financing in California; pundits estimate his castle in San Simeon would cost $500 million in today's dollars. Plans for the Eighth Avenue building did contemplate adding additional floors, and that bit of planning genius turned out to be a serendipitous benefit in our getting approval for the tower seventy years later. But six stories it was at all times until 2006.

At the end of World War II, in 1946, plans were filed for an addition to the Hearst Building. But although the magazine division was expanding, there was no follow-up. Instead, the company began a decades-long process of opening individual offices in other Manhattan buildings. After we started acquiring and launching magazines and other businesses in the 1980s, it became clear that we needed even more space, and we thought that it would be beneficial to get our staff under one roof. But we made do by acquiring a couple of modest buildings in the neighborhood.

Gil Maurer and I started dreaming about a new headquarters building, and talked about it off and on during the 1980s. Gil was an advocate for a new building from the beginning of our partnership. At one point we conducted a competition among several architects and commissioned the "winning" architect to build a model. That model, the vision of architect Kevin Roche, sat in my office for more than a decade. Only when nothing urgent was happening would Gil and I sit around and fantasize about Hearst's new headquarters.

Build a building, or build a company? That wasn't even a question. As trustees we had an obligation to optimize value for the

Hearst Family Trust. And as operating executives we were more interested in building a company than building an architectural icon. No edifice complex here! Further, we weren't willing to undertake a building project without the money in the bank to finish it.

In the freewheeling business environment of the 1980s and 1990s, that made us appear to be retro. Well, in a way we were. We talked about values, about good citizenship, about the quality any building we built would have to be, and we meant it. The message from the executive office was that we were pivoting from our traditional product mix to a more contemporary one, and we wanted to grow with limited financial leverage suitable for a company owned by a trust. And when we'd accomplished that, the Hearst headquarters we wanted would become a reality.

The 1990s saw the major acquisitions and internal start-up businesses we had launched in the 1980s take hold. It was the decade of the ESPN purchase, the acquisition of the *San Antonio Express-News*, and eighteen additional TV stations, and the launch of the *SmartMoney* and *Marie Claire* magazines, among other advances. Revenues more than doubled, and earnings grew by more than 350 percent between 1990 and 2000. Time to talk about that new building.

At first we considered leaving Eighth Avenue and building elsewhere. There was no economic advantage to moving; land costs were higher in other sections of the city. And there was an intriguing and potentially complicating fact about our existing building: only the exterior of the building had been designated by the Landmarks Commission. Could a brilliant architect create an iconic structure by building over the existing building?

At the March 2000 Board of Directors meeting we proposed a

new headquarters building, and I asked for approval to form an architecture committee to find a suitable firm to carry out the plan. Gil Maurer was the obvious choice to chair the committee. He was joined by both management and Hearst Family members of the board, notably W. R. Hearst grandchildren Millicent Hearst Boudjakdji and Austin Hearst, CFO Ron Doerfler, General Counsel Harvey Lipton, Chief Legal and Development Officer Jim Asher, and Cathie Black, president of Hearst Magazines, whose New York–based magazine division would occupy the largest amount of space in the building.

In discussions that followed, critical considerations were debated. Gil, an artist himself and a knowledgeable student of architecture, helped expand the list of possible architects. We shouldn't only interview American architects, he said; architecture is an international language. There were other important considerations. The Hearst Family's name would be on the building, likely for half a century or more. We were a company on the move, and the building had to make a statement: It had to make us proud. And it had to be worth the time and money we'd commit to its creation—we figured it would drain immense energy from other projects for as much as five years. Clearly, a world-class architect would be necessary if we were to achieve those objectives.

Thus began what became known as the Great Hearst Architectural Tour. It had two restrictions: The search could only include winners of the Pritzker Prize—which is widely understood to be the premier prize for architects, effectively the Pulitzer Prize of architecture—and the architect we'd select had to be less than seventy years of age. This project was going to take years, and we wanted someone who'd be alive for the ribbon cutting.

Well, there was a third restriction—a travel budget. I thought I had set one up and later referred to it as "unlimited," but even Gil, a great respecter of the value of a buck in his day job, managed to exceed it.

The search came to an abrupt end when the committee met Norman Foster. They went to Frankfurt, where Foster had designed the Commerzbank, then the tallest building in Europe. And they went to Berlin, where Foster had created the redesign of the Reichstag, using the original building as the base. After that, as Gil has recalled, "There was Norman Foster . . . and everybody else."

I flew to Europe and made the Foster tour myself, with Norman piloting his own plane between the several destinations. It soon became clear that he was as interested in creating a great building in the United States as we were interested in having him design the Hearst Tower. But there was a hurdle, New York City's Landmarks Preservation Commission. Gil relayed a conversation he had with Jennifer Raab, chairwoman of the Landmarks Commission. Her advice: "You've got to knock our socks off." He and I agreed that if anyone could do that it would be Foster.

◆

For a publishing and broadcast executive, I've probably had more firsthand interaction and experience with world-class architects than anyone I can think of. When I succeeded Bill Paley as chairman of the Museum of Broadcasting in 1990, I inherited the responsibility of dealing with the inestimable Philip Johnson as the 52nd Street museum moved to completion. In 1993 to 1996, again in my capacity as chairman of what is now known as the Paley Center for Media, I worked with Richard Meier (who was then finishing the thirteen-year construction of the Getty Museum) on a West Coast facility in Beverly Hills that had been authorized shortly after the New York building had opened. From 2001 until the completion of Hearst Tower, Norman Foster was a regular part of my life. From 2005, when I accepted the chairmanship of Lincoln Center, until the completion of the Lincoln Center Redevelopment Project, Liz Diller of Diller Scofidio+Renfro would dazzle me with its design.

I found all of these architects had in common one characteristic, along with their architectural brilliance: They are superb salespeople—they can communicate as well as they design. Needless to say, Foster was up to the task of "knocking the socks off" the Landmarks Commission as Gil had promised Chairwoman Raab.

For starters, how about this idea? Gut the building. Insert a forty-six-story glass-and-steel tower inside it, with a dramatic atrium that's as big as the building's footprint. And support the building on the exterior with a steel exoskeleton.

The triangle is the strongest shape in architecture. Consider the geodesic dome: it's nearly impossible for even the strongest storm to take it down. As it happened, Buckminster Fuller, the inventor of the geodesic dome, was lecturing at Yale when Norman Foster was studying there. And Norman didn't just file the information about triangles—he was such an enthusiast he had a copy made of one of the few three-wheeled Dymaxion cars that Fuller built.

Norman's exoskeleton would be of steel beams, welded into triangles, with glass inserts—there wouldn't be an ounce of brick or stone on the new tower. This design made it clear that the Tower would have two constituencies. One was the public: to make the exterior of the tower a statement of Hearst's commitment to beautify and inspire our city for the next half century. The other, equally important constituency was Hearst employees: the interior needed to be a statement of Hearst's genuine caring about the two thousand people who would work there.

The triangular steel exoskeleton more than fulfilled the first commitment. As for the second—the inside—instead of a tight little lobby, picture an atrium the size of the building's footprint, with the ceiling soaring seventy feet above the entrance. Outside, the diagrid. Inside, a village square, a piazza, a city in microcosm. And there would be a dramatic viewscape.

In order to make the atrium airy and open, Foster eliminated the central elevator bank that's crucial to the support of traditional buildings and set the elevators at the back of the building, both to keep them from dividing the atrium and as additional support. Then he emphasized the distance between the lobby and the first floor by inserting a fifty-six-foot escalator—an escalator so big it would have to be constructed in one piece, hoisted by crane, lowered into the building, and then installed at a diagonal.

What you wouldn't notice was just as exciting. The triangles would use 20 percent less steel than regular construction, and 90 percent of that steel would be recycled. Heat would be distributed in thermal floors and temperature-controlled walls. There would be a herb garden on the roof.

On both sides of the escalator, there would be Jamie Carpenter's *Ice Falls*, a glass sculpture with cascading steps and endlessly flowing water. Norman pointed out that the water would cool and humidify the atrium. Best of all, the source of the water would be rainfall collected on the roof and stored in a fourteen-thousand-gallon tank below the building. And filling one wall would be Richard Long's *Riverlines*. It wasn't exactly a painting, though it had the rigor of one; khaki-colored sand from the Hudson River and England's River Avon was meticulously layered on a giant canvas.

Foster's Hearst Tower would be the most modern of contrasts with the 1920s Art Deco Hearst Magazine building. I insisted on one throwback feature. The *Good Housekeeping* dining room was the site of numerous important dinners and lunches we hosted with the nation's—actually the world's—political and industrial leaders. I had been there for events with Hubert Humphrey, Gerald Ford, Richard Nixon, Ronald Reagan, George H. W. Bush, Donald Trump, and Margaret Thatcher, along with the CEOs of General Motors, AT&T, and Citibank, to name only a few.

At my request Ellen Levine, then the editor of *Good Housekeeping*, supervised the effort to photograph, measure, and identify every element so as to reconstruct it on the twenty-ninth floor of Hearst Tower. I wanted every detail in that space to look just as it had for generations of guests and Hearst executives in the Art Deco original building. I love the history it evokes, and we still have board lunches there after every Hearst Board meeting.

Foster's concept and the quality of his pitch were electrifying. But the new Hearst Tower would be just a gleam in our collective eyes unless the Landmarks Preservation Commission blessed the plan. Gil Maurer again had an idea. There was a small empty store on the first floor. Collecting rent was a much lower priority than having a design studio where we could have monthly meetings with members of the commission. We could host creative, give-and-take sessions there; we could make the commission our collaborators. We established a development office in that empty store and met with commission members there. They would suggest small changes; most of the time we were happy to agree. Soon there were no more points to negotiate.

I don't recall cheering when we got not only the go-ahead but also a rare unanimous vote of the Landmarks Preservation Commission, though I must have had trouble restraining myself. As a salesman I learned long ago that when you get the order you act as if it was never in doubt, and, importantly, you leave immediately.

The most memorable day of all is seared in my memory, as I know is the case with my associates who were present. We scheduled a meeting for the Hearst Board to review the Foster plan on September 12, 2001. Norman flew in early and came to our offices on the morning of September 11 to rehearse for the next day's meeting. And there we sat, silent in my conference room, watching the towers of the World Trade Center fall. We thought the towers would fall over sideways. Norman correctly predicted the heat would cause them to collapse straight down. In the aftermath, we thought all the things everyone did, but in addition our thought process included wondering if anyone would be willing to build our Tower, any tower, ever again in New York. Our board members from out of town were unable to get into New York, and there was no meeting on September 12.

We managed our business and supported our employees through the horrors of the aftermath of 9/11. We were soon to be resolute. Neither my management colleagues nor our board were about to let "those bastards" dictate the future of New York, the USA, or Hearst. By the end of October, we had decided to go ahead with the project. I think that decision by our Board of Directors—an unreserved expression of faith in the city's future, and ours as a company—goes down as one of the most courageous and committed decisions any board ever made. My colleagues and I took numerous risks in the process of rebuilding Hearst. We had our necks out pretty far in urging the board to stay the course and build Hearst Tower.

The board also decided that our little company was doing just fine, thank you, and we could do the unheard-of thing: avoid the traditional bank or insurance company financing of New York buildings by writing a check every time one was required during construction, just as you would do if remodeling your kitchen. In effect, we'd own the best home in town—without a mortgage.

The Tower was completed in 2006. It instantly won a LEED (Leadership in Energy and Environmental Design) Gold designation—the first commercial building in New York City to have one. Later, the LEED designation was upgraded to Platinum.

Gil Maurer justifiably is often referred to in this narrative. His contribution was singular, but others deserve and have the gratitude of all of us for making Hearst Tower what it is today. Cathie Black spent endless hours and contributed a great deal to the amenities and functionality. The late Ron Doerfler, our chief financial officer at the time, probably spent the most time of anyone in overseeing the numerous details of construction, funding, and contractor oversight. Jim Asher, our chief legal and development officer, was often at Ron's side. Jerry Speyer, CEO of Tishman Speyer, and his associates guided us flawlessly through construction decisions and complexities for which we had little or no competency. Two of Foster's associates, Brandon Haw and Michael Wurzel, were so important to the project and so responsive to us that they remain friends to whom we regularly express our appreciation.

I stepped down from the CEO role less than a year after we got the project officially underway, but I stayed with it, attended every meeting, and provided input on every decision until completion. My successor CEO, Victor Ganzi, gave every detail of the project his complete and undivided attention, and did so with good humor and skill. He didn't start the project, but he had as much to do with successfully completing its construction as anyone.

Norman Foster loves the building so much he's rented half a floor from us; the Tower is his American headquarters. He experiences what we do: When every desk in these open-plan offices drinks in the view of the great city of New York, you can't help but feel energized and optimistic.

That is exactly what we dreamed. And, I would like to think, exactly what William Randolph Hearst would have wanted.

CHAPTER 14

Giving Back, or How Do You Get to Lincoln Center? Practice!

There must be a national network of pro bono executives, because as soon as I moved from San Antonio to New York, the causes I'd supported in Texas wanted my help in my new home. In my seven years as publisher of the *San Antonio Light*, that pro bono commitment had included engagement with United Way, board membership at the predominantly female and Hispanic Our Lady of the Lake University, chairmanships of the Chamber of Commerce, the San Antonio Symphony/Opera, and the Alamo Area Council of Boy Scouts of America, among others. In New York, the leaders of those organizations, or closely related organizations, pounced on me like a fumbled football.

What didn't travel north with me, happily, was word of my tennis match against Bobby Riggs. I'll repeat that while you realign your jaw: I played Bobby Riggs. Does it count if it was for the benefit of a local boys home? Well, it does in my house.

It happened in 1973, not long after the flamboyant Riggs defeated the world's number one women's player, Margaret Court, in the infamous "Mother's Day Massacre," and shortly before the highly publicized "Battle of the Sexes" match with Billie Jean King in the Astrodome. It escapes me now how I got roped into it, but it was decided that among that evening's attractions I needed to swallow my pride and take on the former world's number one. Not alone, thank the Lord. Dan Cook—the popular TV sports anchor and sports editor of the *San Antonio Express-News*, then our competitor newspaper—and I, publisher of the *Light*, would take the court in an exhibition match against Riggs.

Cook and I were fair weekend tennis players, not that our skill levels mattered. But we wanted to make Riggs break a sweat, so we played a couple of practice sessions and worked out with the Trinity University women's team. The Trinity women at that time were among the best in the college ranks and in the world amateur standings—it wasn't disgraceful that we didn't exactly distinguish ourselves against them.

We cheered up slightly as we took the court: Riggs was dressed in a brightly colored muumuu and carrying a valise. These were intended to constitute handicaps, but Riggs hardly let either of us get a shot past him. When I did—just once, with my kids as my cheering squad—Riggs mumbled an expletive and introduced me to a game I did not know existed: He placed several chairs on his side of the net. The deal was that he dared us to win a point by hitting one of the chairs before he could get to the ball to execute his always sizzling return.

Living up to his reputation as a huckster, Riggs brought along a supply of silver coins with a pig image on one side, and the wording "Male Chauvinist Pig" on the other. I think he charged $20 per coin, and he got it from numerous takers, including me. I noted with amusement that particular fundraising went into his pocket rather than the charity.

◆

Those early days in New York had me plenty busy, and I was also on the road a lot. That made living up to my longtime commitment to give back to the community substantially more challenging. I already had one significant pro bono cause: John Miller thought it necessary that I follow him and our predecessors by engaging with United Cerebral Palsy.

In the mid-1980s, Bruce Crawford, whom I had come to know as chief executive officer of the advertising agency BBDO, became general manager of the Metropolitan Opera. He asked me to chair a Met fundraiser, which I did. In 1989, also at his urging, I joined the Board of Managing Directors, as the opera's governing body is called. I've served in that capacity ever since, also serving on the Executive Committee and as chair of the Audit Committee.

It's a fairly well-known shibboleth around New York that "Any call from Frank Bennack is a collect call." But despite my love of the Met Opera and my steady engagement in its governance, I have somehow been able to avoid the role as a principal fundraiser that I have played from time to time at my other pro bono institutions.

Contributor yes, fundraiser no.

One of my Met colleagues, himself a big supporter, once said, "The only thing more expensive than Grand Opera is war." That comes close to being true. But I believe that the preservation of that magnificent art form is essential to a cultured society. It's also, in worldlier terms, very good for the New York economy. More than seven million people a year make it a point to visit the Lincoln Center campus, and the largest of the campus organizations, by far, is the Metropolitan Opera.

Curiously, the civic pride of offering the spectacular performances of the greatest opera company in the world doesn't seem to resonate at the Met in the same way that civic pride drives philanthropic support for Lincoln Center as a whole, or the city's primary museums. The Met box office accounts for less than 40 percent of what is needed to fund an opera season. The rest has to be raised from other sources, including an approximate $140 to $150 million annually from donors. And these supporters—at least the major ones, it seems to me—for the most part are true opera lovers, as contrasted to the civic boosters who make up the base of support for many New York cultural treasures.

Their willingness to step up time and again is something I marvel at; thank God for them. And let me heap praise on Peter Gelb, the brilliant general manager of the Met, who has given us numerous beloved traditional classics and an increased menu of new and creative productions, season after season.

A prime example: the 2018/19 season's opening night performance of Camille Saint-Saëns's *Samson et Dalila*. I've been going to the opera for more than fifty years; the final act of this production may well be the most spectacular I have ever seen. First, the drama of more and more people streaming onstage, until there were more than a hundred. Then the effects: smoke and fire. And, above all, the beautiful music. My ultimate judgment for entertainment—you're experiencing something you can find nowhere else—is more than satisfied here.

In September of 1994, Beverly Sills, the new chair of Lincoln Center for the Performing Arts, asked me to add the Lincoln Center board to my board service at the Met Opera. Interestingly, in 1981 Gil Maurer and I had talked to Beverly about becoming editor of *Connoisseur*, a British magazine we planned to launch in the United States. She toyed with the idea but eventually passed on the opportunity, and we appointed Tom Hoving to that post.

Hearst ran at top speed in the 1990s. We acquired the *San Antonio Express-News*, and went through the painful process of closing my old shop, the *San Antonio Light*. We bought out minority partners in our A&E and Lifetime cable networks and consolidated our holdings of those cable services with our partners, Cap Cities/ABC. In 1990 we acquired our 20 percent stake in ESPN. In that decade we launched ten magazines and acquired nineteen of the thirty-three TV stations Hearst owns today, including ten from the successor company of W. R. Hearst's fiercest competitor at the turn of the twentieth century, headed by Joseph Pulitzer. A favorite moment was when Michael Pulitzer, a surviving son of Joseph Pulitzer, and I shook hands on the transaction. With a wry smile, he said, "As to the goings-on at the turn of the twentieth century, all is forgiven."

This nonstop activity meant that about all I could do for the Met and Lincoln Center was show up at board meetings, provide personal financial support, and recommend Hearst's continued financial support. It simply wasn't feasible to take a genuine leadership role. It is testimony to the persuasiveness of Beverly Sills that she convinced me to serve on a long-range planning committee and to chair the search committee for a new Lincoln Center president.

◆

From the mid-1990s until 2001 Lincoln Center leadership encouraged me to think about a time when I might consider taking on the chairmanship. It was pretty clear to me that while I would be honored to devote myself to this vital institution, I really couldn't think about that while still in the CEO chair at Hearst. For one thing Beverly's long-range planning committee had identified hundreds of millions in funds that had to be raised to bring this unique treasure up to modern standards, and her successor would surely have to take the lead in planning and funding what became known as Redevelopment. Beverly had skillfully, with the help of Gordon Davis, a prominent attorney who had served in New York City administrations going back to John Lindsay and had been a highly successful Parks Commissioner, convinced the Rudolph Giuliani administration that the City of New York needed to fund about a quarter of a billion dollars. The private sector would need to contribute the rest of a projected billion-dollar-plus undertaking. No performing arts center anywhere had ever undertaken a project of that magnitude.

Over time a few events influenced my changing perspective and a different outcome. In 2002, in consultation with my senior associates at Hearst, I decided that twenty-three years as CEO was enough. I was far from burned-out, but new leadership would bring new thinking and new energy. Gil Maurer, with whom I had always consulted about my tenure, said I needed to consider how long my likely successor, Victor Ganzi, would stick around as number two. The Company was performing at a level beyond anything we had dreamed. We had significantly diversified and grown revenue more than sevenfold and earnings at a rate double that.

It seemed a good time for me to move to a consultative role, and continue to influence the Company's affairs but not manage them day-to-day. Luella was longing for us to spend more time near our children and grandchildren in Texas, but she agreed I could stay around New York enough to do this scaled-down job—and no more. So on June 30, 2002, I passed the baton to Ganzi, my carefully selected and personally trained chief operating officer. I technically retired as an active employee but stayed engaged as vice chairman of the board and chairman of the Executive Committee. And I retained my status as a trustee of the Hearst Family Trust, a lifetime appointment.

Somewhat surprisingly, also in 2002, Beverly Sills decided to step down as chair of Lincoln Center. She immediately assumed the same role at the Metropolitan Opera. This left a relatively new Lincoln Center president, Reynold ("Ren") Levy, without a successor chairman and with the heavy burden of the early stages of "Bravo Lincoln Center," the name given to the fundraising campaign launched in connection with Redevelopment. Because I had chaired the search committee that found and employed Levy, some attention turned to the prospect of my taking the role.

Luella's plan for a reduced New York schedule didn't seem ideal for an affirmative response.

Bruce Crawford, who had made an unexcelled contribution to the Met Opera, and who was especially close to Beverly, agreed to assume the chairmanship for an undetermined but limited time. This was the best possible outcome; absolutely nobody was Crawford's equal in the gravitas, preparation, and skills required for the job at that precise time, and it was an act of pure civic responsibility that guided his decision to say yes. I was pleased to serve Crawford as chair of a Finance Committee, which, believe it or not, had not existed previously at Lincoln Center.

Tragically and totally without warning, on April 17, 2003, Luella died in our San Antonio condo from an aortic dissection. Our youngest daughter, Julie, and I had just arrived from New York. It was Holy Thursday, and our family had started to gather for our traditional Easter Holiday break at our Texas ranch. All of our lives were suddenly turned upside down. What now?

Beverly Sills would qualify in any life she touched as one of the most remarkable people ever encountered. By the time she recruited me to the Lincoln Center Board, in addition to her challenges of looking after two significantly handicapped children, she had been confronted with her beloved husband Peter's massive stroke. And yet any interaction with her included the lifting of your spirits—she wasn't called "Bubbles" for nothing.

Both before and after Luella's death Beverly and I were great pals. Like everyone else I don't think I ever turned down any request she made of me. At her memorial service years later I used a line I originally applied to John Connally: "Beverly Sills can talk a dog off of a meat truck."

In the fall of 2003, I was suffering mightily and keeping sane by working harder than ever, and not doing much else except spending time with my kids, mostly with Julie, our only child in New York. As opening night of the opera season and the Met's glorious annual gala approached, I got a message on my voicemail from Beverly: "Mr. Bennack, this is Beverly Sills. I am aware that you have always attended the Met Opera's opening night gala. This year you are going to be my escort, and I require a corsage." I was her escort, and my presence at the Met was never more taken note of, and I did my homework and ordered a wrist corsage, Beverly's preference.

◆

Reynold Levy, one of the brightest and most able managers I've ever worked with, in and out of the pro bono world, and the ring-wise Bruce Crawford got "Bravo Lincoln Center" underway. Crawford insisted on a certain level of fundraising before the Redevelopment project was a "go" and, therefore, before any construction could begin. Between them they recruited a skilled and committed team of employees and volunteer leaders. But a project of this size and scope had never been accomplished before. Maybe it wasn't possible.

Everyone who signed on as a support cast attended a series of meetings where the plans were unveiled, debated, and ultimately unanimously approved. Incredibly, rules established for governance that required unanimous approval of every organization's element were somehow adhered to. While there were some cost overruns, the major increases from the original targets were more the result of "scope expansions," new elements sought by the individual organizations—in this world, they're called "constituents"—and were the natural consequence of a process in which every affirmative vote was needed for every plan enhancement. In the West, where I come from, that's called horse-trading. There's politics everywhere; some would argue more in the pro bono world than anywhere.

Crawford and Levy recruited Bruce Kovner, chairman of the board of Juilliard, to chair the first phase of the project and to undertake the tedious process of getting the unanimous agreement needed to keep the process moving. Kovner is both an extraordinarily skilled businessman and negotiator, as his success in creating and managing the hedge fund CAM Capital (formerly Caxton) indicated, and he is also a world-class authority on all things musical. Later, during my tenure as chair, Ren Levy identified Dan Brodsky, a real estate developer on the Ballet board, as the person to fill a similar leadership role as chair of the Josie Robertson Plaza group, as the second phase of the project was called. I enthusiastically concurred, and Brodsky adroitly displayed the diplomatic skill required in guiding those discussions to final approval.

There were a small number of notable detractors who thought the entire process unnecessary or too costly, but most constituents were ardent supporters. A redeveloped Lincoln Center began to look more than possible, and there was genuine excitement on campus.

By 2004 Crawford started to talk to me about succession. I had stepped down as CEO of Hearst, and it no longer seemed likely that I was going to return to Texas on anything approaching a full-time basis. I wasn't personally ready to take the job on, so he and I explored and pitched other potential candidates. Crawford wanted to turn the reins over the following year at the latest.

Meanwhile, I continued to give Hearst a full day's work.

On April 2, 2005, two years after Luella's death, I married Dr. Mary Lake Polan, a nationally known reproductive endocrinologist, physician leader, and, for sixteen years, distinguished chair of Obstetrics and Gynecology at Stanford University. We had gotten to know each other by virtue of our joint service on the board of the Wyeth Corporation. The Opera again entered the picture in quite a different way. After associates at Wyeth had worked to play matchmaker by getting Mary Lake and me together in various ways, I decided I could handle matters myself. Much too late for a polite invitation, I decided to call Mary Lake in California to invite her to the opening night performance and gala of the 2004/05 Met Opera season. She accepted, and soon accepted a longer-term invitation.

Remarkably, Mary Lake agreed to move to New York after our marriage in return for a tongue-in-cheek pledge that we would have no more children—we have eight between us—and that she wouldn't ever have to cook again. Cooking or no cooking, Mary Lake was taking on a range of motherly and grandmotherly roles. My five daughters and, at the time, ten grandchildren came with the bargain. My own parental duties didn't exactly get smaller. For the first time I had two welcome sons, Joshua and Scott, and Lindsay, who was Mary Lake's only child I had met when I proposed marriage, gave me a sixth loving and lovable daughter.

I've seldom used the term "step" to distinguish our children.

Importantly, Mary Lake thought it would be good if I accepted Crawford's entreaties to become chairman of Lincoln Center. I spoke with Gil Maurer, Vic Ganzi, and George Hearst Jr., and they all encouraged me to accept. I remember Gil saying that with the exception of running for mayor, which he knew I wasn't about to do, helping make the Lincoln Center project a success was the highest civic contribution I could make. Deal!

◆

There are two main areas where a "civilian" chairman can add real value to capable full-time professional management: (1) relationships with the constituents, particularly relationships with constituent board chairs, and (2) fundraising. Oh yes, fundraising.

The huge construction aspects of Redevelopment actually

added a third major responsibility to the list of chair priorities I had envisioned. Katherine Farley, a senior executive in the worldwide real estate firm Tishman Speyer, who had started her career as an architect and project coordinator at Turner Construction, took over leadership of the Lincoln Center Redevelopment Project. I was thrilled because I knew the skill with which she would handle that enormous task—and because, along with others, I felt she was a leading candidate to succeed me as chair of Lincoln Center, which she did. This was especially comfortable because Katherine's amazing husband, Jerry Speyer, was instrumental in the successful planning and construction of Hearst Tower, and he and I had clearly bonded. It wouldn't be out of the question if one were to observe that among my greatest achievements was getting both members of this power couple to work on my behalf at the same time.

David Rubenstein, cofounder of the massive Washington, D.C., private equity firm The Carlyle Group, has probably raised as much money as anybody on the planet. Ren and I recruited him to chair the "Bravo Lincoln Center" capital campaign. David was a great partner, and great fun.

We very quickly developed an irresistible pitch. We'd known the potential donors for years, and our meetings invariably began with personal stories about our families and friends. As appropriate, we shared business developments and our thoughts about the city and the economy. In that relaxed conversation, it wasn't awkward to make the case for supporting Lincoln Center.

One thing I never failed to mention: While I was CEO, the Hearst Corporation was the first to announce a new headquarters in New York after the attack on 9/11. When I stepped down as

CEO, I concluded that being the chairman of Lincoln Center at this exciting time in its history would be the next important role I could play—nothing of its size, diversity, and quality in the performing arts exists in any one place anywhere else.

And then . . . the ask: "New York City is on board with the commitment of $240 million. New York State and the federal government have each pledged $30 million. That leaves in excess of $700 million to be raised privately, and we expect the board of directors of Lincoln Center to unanimously participate and to collectively donate the critical mass of that sum.

"I am here this morning to ask you to please consider joining me and Hearst with a leadership gift of no less than $5 million.

"You will not ever regret being a major part of this rejuvenation of a singular set of institutions. It is early in our campaign. But so far no one has turned us down. Please do not be the first to do so."

For those of you who are ever tasked with fundraising, I'd point out that there's nothing flashy about my approach. I make a personal connection, I describe the need, and then I ask for the money—very much like a high school debater. There is one area where experience comes into play: The first person I ask for money is a CEO I know well. I tell him/her what Hearst has committed. And I say, "If you say yes, everyone else will." Which is exactly what happened.

◆

A highlight of my five years as chair of Lincoln Center was the support I got from the constituent chairs. Bill Morris of the Met, Bruce Kovner of Juilliard, Susan Baker and Marty Oppenheimer of the New York City Opera, Paul Guenther and Gary Parr of the Philharmonic, Linda Janklow of Lincoln Center Theater, Ann Tenenbaum of the Film Society, Barry Friedberg of the New York City Ballet, Lisa Schiff of Jazz at Lincoln Center, Peter Frelinghuysen of the Chamber Music Society, and Elizabeth Rohatyn on behalf of the Library of the Performing Arts conscientiously showed up at the meetings of constituent chairs I regularly hosted. They offered both support and advice, and by advice, often that meant "complaints."

A change of scenery is often both welcome and useful. A good representation of the constituent chairs and their spouses joined Katherine Farley and Jerry Speyer, Ren and Liz Levy, and Mary Lake and me for a weekend at our Texas ranch. The goal was to build trust, the essential ingredient in creating agreements. So I invited all constituent chairs and their spouses or partners for weekend trips to my Texas ranch. We offered many diversions: hiking, skeet shooting, riding. And then we got together around the barbecue pit. Most of our guests already knew one another, but friendships deepened.

Back in New York, two remarkable and brilliant women delivered creative solutions to other obstacles and earned both my gratitude and admiration.

Liz Diller was an inspired choice to lead the architectural challenges of Redevelopment. I wish I could take even a little credit for having chosen her and her firm, but they were already in place when I assumed the chairmanship. The result of her architectural magic is now there for the whole world to see and admire.

Despite the constant pressure to keep on fundraising, we hit a wall from time to time. In fact, one of the most remarkable aspects of the entire campaign is the number of donors who said yes two, three, and even four times over the life of the project. The structure that would become Lincoln, the restaurant covered with the uniquely imaginative Tisch Illumination Lawn roof, was among the most costly individual elements in the entire architectural scheme. It was also, in Liz's view, among the most important, a signature design element. At one juncture when it appeared that the fundraising and project costs might not align, it became necessary to look for ways to manage down our expenses.

Should we think about scrapping the restaurant? Ren and I assembled a leadership group and invited Liz to come and explain how damaging the removal of the restaurant would be.

She made an excellent case for the restaurant as an indispensable element of her design. I don't think Liz breathed as members asked questions or made rebuttals. When everyone had weighed in, Ren and I walked over to the side of the room and looked each other squarely in the eye. "It stays," we said almost in unison. We've had no reason to regret that decision. Lincoln Ristorante has been a success as a restaurant, and contributes uniquely to what Liz envisioned as the beauty of the new Lincoln Center campus.

Another key player who gained my robust and continuing admiration was Amanda Burden, director of the New York City Department of City Planning and chair of the City Planning Commission under Mayor Michael Bloomberg. The nature of our project was such that we required regular consultation with, and approval of, City Planning. I had learned in my prior interaction with Amanda in the early planning for the Hearst

Tower project that she treated every proposed project as if it were in her backyard and that she would be held forever responsible for the outcome. My associates on both projects, perhaps particularly at Lincoln Center, might wish for me to be more measured, as there were tense moments and differences of opinion at various junctures. Amanda Burden was as inspired and positive an influence on Lincoln Center Redevelopment as she and Jennifer Raab at Landmarks had been on Hearst Tower. And I am grateful. Michael Bloomberg, as mayor of New York City and as a private citizen–philanthropist, was indispensable to the success of Lincoln Center redevelopment.

◆

One story summarizes my experience as Lincoln Center chair. Ronald Stanton, a generous businessman who had achieved great success as founder of Transammonia, Inc., now called Trammo, was an early contributor to "Bravo Lincoln Center." I knew him well as a result of his philanthropy elsewhere in the city, specifically at NewYork-Presbyterian Hospital. We had reached one of those junctures in "Bravo Lincoln Center"—we needed a kick-start to the campaign, and it needed to be sizable in order to reenergize us all.

Ren and I talked about Stanton as a possible prospect who just might give us what we needed with an additional gift. We had learned that Martin Segal, perhaps the best-recognized modern-day chairman of Lincoln Center, had a particularly close association with Stanton. We conferred with Marty and persuaded him to join us in the solicitation. We made the appointment at the Four Seasons Hotel, where Stanton often had lunch. During the main course Ren and I started to make our case. Out of left field, Marty

Segal said, "Ron, we need for you to give us $25 million." Stanton didn't blink. "Do I have to pay it all at once?" he replied. When I recovered, I said something like "Over two or three years will be just fine, Ron."

Only in New York! At times like that I'm reminded of what P. T. Barnum is reputed to have said, "There's only one New York; all else is Bridgeport." Barnum could say that; I can't, because we at Hearst proudly claim the *Connecticut Post* as one of Hearst's twenty-four daily and sixty-three weekly newspapers. It serves Bridgeport with distinction.

CHAPTER 15

The Presidents I've Known

I've previously suggested that my tenure as publisher of my hometown newspaper, the *San Antonio Light*, was a job that could never be improved upon. Except, as I think about it, in one way—had I stayed in that role, the incredibly rich experiences of meeting every president of the United States since Eisenhower, except JFK, and meeting many private sector presidents and captains of industry would never have been possible.

In 1956, when Dwight Eisenhower was running for reelection, he came to campaign in San Antonio, the site of Fort Sam Houston, where Ike had served decades earlier and met his wife. In those days San Antonio was not the friendliest of cities for Republicans. I recall a sign in the *Light*'s composing room that boldly stated:

BEN HOGAN FOR PRESIDENT. IF YOU WANT A GOLFER FOR PRESIDENT, GET A GOOD ONE!

Ike was appearing at a rally at the McCreless Market Shopping Center, a relatively new San Antonio mall and the first to be built in the South Side neighborhood where I grew up. Earlier that year I had returned to the newspaper from my tour in Europe with the Army. I was impressed that the legendary general, who had commanded the European Theater where I had served, was coming to my hometown.

The fabled Eisenhower smile was truly memorable. Some thought he was a less-than-talented orator, but this former schoolboy orator found Ike's stump speech compelling.

After the formal electioneering speeches concluded, Ike stood around, as I recall it, exchanging pleasantries. I worked my way up to tell the president that I had only recently returned from the Europe he and his joint forces had liberated and saved. He actually seemed interested and signed a copy of the rally brochure for me, again flashing that infectious smile.

That encounter likely contributed to the warm and admiring feelings I developed for the thirty-fourth president. Those feelings for the person Ike was and the record he established of balanced budgets were very persuasive to me. That his administration established the national interstate highway system was also important, particularly since the Hearst newspapers' support was critical to the success of that initiative. All of this causes me to conclude that Eisenhower might just be the most underrated president in modern American history.

The late Bob Considine, who would rank as one of the most talented reporter/columnists in the history of the Hearst Newspapers, interviewed the retired former president years after my encounter. According to Considine, he said something like this to the aging Ike: "President Eisenhower, during the course of your life you have commanded at D-Day, arguably the greatest aggregation of military might in history. You experienced a grateful people twice electing you president of the greatest nation in history, and by landslides. You served as president of Columbia, one of the nation's most distinguished universities. What else could you possibly aspire to be?"

Ike's response: "My grandson, David."

◆

On November 21, 1963, the day before he was assassinated in Dallas, John F. Kennedy visited San Antonio. I wasn't senior enough to have been invited to any meet-and-greet events, but everyone at the *Light* had the opportunity to see JFK close-up as his motorcade passed a few feet from our building. All *Light* personnel were excited and felt as if the president had visited them.

I was miles away at the Wonderland Mall doing my duty as an ad salesman, calling on a senior Montgomery Ward executive to ensure we, rather than the competition, got the largest share of Montgomery Ward advertising. I always regretted that sales call. Probably the only sales call I ever wished I hadn't made. The picture that ran in our paper the Saturday morning after the Friday assassination was taken from the window of the publisher's office I would later occupy.

I did, however, spend a particularly memorable New York City evening with Jacqueline Kennedy Onassis in 1990, when she was a book editor.

Pierre Salinger, JFK's press secretary, had gone on to fashion a distinguished career as ABC bureau chief in Paris and as the network's chief European correspondent. The Museum of Television & Radio decided to do a day-long tribute to Salinger, both because of his importance in American politics and his accomplishments as a journalist.

At an afternoon session, one of Salinger's ABC colleagues asked him to explain how, as press secretary, he handled questions about JFK's extramarital affairs. Salinger replied, at some length, that he and his associates were able to keep the press at bay by suggesting that Kennedy, as president in trying times, was simply too busy to have such activities on the side. And the press, almost without exception great fans of JFK, had essentially left the story alone.

That evening the museum hosted a celebratory dinner in honor of Salinger and landed not only Arthur Schlesinger Jr. and Ted Sorensen but also Jacqueline Kennedy Onassis as attendees.

The evening started with a mini-version of the afternoon Q&A with Pierre Salinger. I had become chairman of the museum after William Paley's death that year, so it was my duty and pleasure to meet the former first lady in the lobby and escort her to the assigned location in the theater. We were to make a dramatic walk down the aisle to our seats, but just as we arrived at the door of the two-hundred-seat theater, somebody in the audience—I think it was the same guy who had raised the subject earlier—asked Salinger to tell the story about handling JFK's affairs.

The expression on Mrs. Onassis's face did not change as we waited at the door for the answer, which was the same as Salinger's story at the afternoon session.

I walked a stoic Jacqueline Kennedy down the aisle, and we took our seats in a hushed theater.

After the Q&A session we all headed for dinner. At our table were Schlesinger, Sorensen, Salinger, museum president Bob Batscha, Mrs. Onassis on my right, and Luella on my left. I had a delightful dinner conversation with Mrs. Onassis, who, in her almost childlike voice that belied her age, was asking me question after question about book, magazine, and newspaper publishing. Later it came time for introductions and speeches. I leaned over to Salinger and said, "Pierre, I know what I'm going to say about Schlesinger, Mrs. Onassis, and obviously, about you. But what should I say about Ted Sorensen?"

"You could say that most of the great and memorable lines uttered by JFK were written by Ted," Salinger said.

Jackie—I guess by this time I can call her that—grabbed my arm and said, loud enough for the entire table to hear, "Don't you dare say that. My husband wrote most of those memorable lines himself."

Others might view that event differently, but I've remembered it as a demonstration of both class and loyalty, if I ever witnessed it. This was a woman who had faced the embarrassment of a discussion about her husband's affairs and was now militantly standing up for that husband's legacy and role in history.

◆

Lyndon Baines Johnson, the nation's thirty-sixth president, effectively had three hometown newspapers: the *Austin American-Statesman*, the *San Antonio Express-News*, and our *San Antonio Light*. My understanding was that we at the *Light* might have been his favorite because my predecessors had endorsed and presumably helped elect Johnson in the often revisited "landslide" senatorial election of 1948.

Additionally, corporate legend has it that Dick Berlin (who was, after the founder, my longest-tenured CEO predecessor at

Hearst) had allowed the Johnson family out of a costly wire service contract with the Hearst-owned International News Service (INS). Lady Bird had acquired an Austin radio station that she found unnecessarily burdened with contracts with all three wire services, AP, UP, and INS. Berlin allowed a cost-free cancellation of INS, so the story goes.

Although most observers thought of the Austin broadcast businesses as being owned by the Johnson family, and ultimately I believe they were, Lady Bird was the legal owner of radio station KTBC and the TV station with the same call letters. She used some of the $21 million from her inheritance, left over after helping fund LBJ's political campaigns, to invest in the radio station in 1942.

Partly through the good graces of Dick Berlin, cousin John Connally, and my valued friend Tom Johnson, I always got easy access to President Johnson, particularly after he returned to his Texas ranch in 1969. By then I was publisher of the *Light*. President Johnson, Lady Bird, and the entire Johnson family befriended me, despite LBJ having plenty of criticism for some of what we wrote about him in our newspaper.

I have too many LBJ stories to recount here, but I'll indulge myself with two or three.

As publisher of the *Light*, I established a regular routine of early morning meetings with the heads of each of the major newspaper departments, editorial, advertising, circulation, and production. This practice was the genesis of the group meetings I initiated in New York after becoming CEO of Hearst.

One morning my always protective assistant, Fran Findebach, called me out of a meeting to tell me that President Johnson was on the phone.

"Frank, it's Lyndon Johnson."

"Good morning, President Johnson," I calmly replied.

"Frank, old friend, I have something I want to talk to you about, and it's something you can't tell anyone."

"President Johnson, you know what business I'm in; I don't think I can give you that assurance without knowing the nature of what it is you wish to tell me," I said, while running through my mind all sorts of things with which he might complicate my life by telling me.

"You'll understand when you hear me out," he said in a low and almost conspiratorial voice.

Sixty seconds of silence that felt like an hour followed.

"Frank, can you send a reporter and photographer up to Stonewall [a small Texas town near the LBJ Ranch] to cover their annual Peach Festival?"

"President Johnson, if it's helpful I'll send two reporters and photographers," I quickly responded, relieved and elated at not being entrusted with the nation's deepest secrets.

My memory isn't clear on exactly what LBJ said after my acquiescence. Recalling that he could use some pretty colorful language, it might have gone something like this: "If the media like the *New York Times* or *Washington Post* find out I'm pimping for a peach festival, God knows what they might print."

I later found out he made the same call to Charles Kilpatrick, publisher of our then rival *Express-News*, who also sent his staffers to Stonewall.

Second story: When Hearst CEO Dick Berlin made a rare visit to San Antonio to participate in the 1970 press launch, he asked that we arrange a visit for him with "Lyndon," as Berlin called him. Incidentally, I wouldn't in a million years have gotten the courage to call LBJ "Lyndon."

I made the arrangements, and Dick, his successor-to-be Frank Massi, and I drove the roughly sixty-five miles from San Antonio to the LBJ Ranch. We were directed to Johnson's bedroom, where he was resting after a recent flare-up of the heart problems he had experienced since he had been in the Senate. I remember vividly that he was hooked up with one of those devices that provide oxygen through a plastic line clipped to the nose. As soon as he saw us, he whipped it out.

While greeting us, and mumbling about the inconvenience of such treatments, he rolled out of the bed in the altogether, slipped on a pair of blue jeans, and announced, "Dick, you've never been here before, and the Bennack kid and I are going to show you and your little associate"—Massi was probably about five foot four— "around the greatest spot on earth." Massi's eyes were as big as saucers at the sight.

And, boy, did LBJ show us around.

Behind the wheel of one of his storied Lincoln sedans, LBJ held in one hand a two-way radio to communicate with ranch personnel as he drove at an uncomfortable speed across the open fields. He inquired about the status of ranch chores, making sure we understood that he was a bona fide, fully engaged rancher. We soon learned that there was another inquiry forthcoming.

The Johnsons by this time not only owned an Austin radio station but a valuable TV station. LBJ was taking advantage of three media "experts" in his presence to ascertain the value of the Austin TV holdings, which the Johnsons would sell to Times Mirror in 1973.

Berlin is thought by some to have saved the Company during the Great Depression. During his presidency of Hearst he had authorized only the purchase of *Popular Mechanics* magazine in 1958 and partial interest in a Pittsburgh television station. Now he was sitting in the front seat alongside LBJ. Although I didn't interpret what transpired in the same way, Berlin apparently thought the former president was attempting to convince him to consider buying KTBC-TV.

Berlin was carrying a little Minox, the tiny camera used to record espionage activities in World War II. He was recording our day at the ranch at every turn.

"Dick, what do you think that our TV station in Austin is worth?" Johnson would inquire, turning his head toward Berlin with only a loose left hand on the wheel.

"Excuse me, Lyndon, I want to take a picture of that bull over there," Berlin would reply, pointing the Minox out the car window while ignoring LBJ's question.

Later, LBJ, not ever one to be denied, followed up: "Dick, do you think an Austin station would be worth as much as the San Antonio station that recently sold?"

"Excuse me, Lyndon. That's a beautiful scene over there that I want to take a picture of to show Honey" (Berlin's wife).

This parrying and fencing went on for the duration of our ride in the Lincoln; to my amazement LBJ, the consummate persuader, never laid a glove on Berlin. My predecessors at Hearst believed Berlin to be the most politically skilled of corporate leaders, and this experience certainly ratified that assessment for me.

At one point LBJ turned his head further still to ask me in the back seat what I thought was the value of the station. I politely asked about its pretax cash flow. Getting the answer, I applied a market multiple, telling President Johnson what my ballpark estimate of value would be. I don't remember what the numbers were, but I likely would have applied a multiple of 12 or so against cash flow.

Johnson: "Dick, did you hear that? Do you know how smart that kid you have running San Antonio is? He's going far, and you better hold on to him."

"Excuse me, Lyndon," Berlin said, "I want to get this shot."

Some months later LBJ entered the hospital at Brooke Army Medical Center at Fort Sam Houston in San Antonio with another heart flare-up. At that time the *Light* employed an award-winning medical reporter, Marjorie Clapp. In this instance Marjorie wrote a thoroughly researched story that compared the excellent care the former president was getting at the Army center to the cost of that care at a top civilian hospital.

LBJ didn't like the story one little bit! The message the story conveyed was, he said, "designed to make it seem like I'm on the public dole, a freeloader."

I tried to persuade him that he had gotten the wrong slant, that the story was designed to convey the message that our beloved, native-son former president was getting the best care money could buy, and that is what all of us would want!

I thought he bought my explanation but he continued to upbraid me: "I've been up here in this damned hospital only a few miles from your office, and I haven't heard a peep out of you. Only Marjorie Clapp and her cheapskate Johnson story."

Recognizing that getting too worked up was not the best state of mind for a man with serious heart issues, I said something about remaining calm, and countered with: "I wasn't sure you were receiving visitors, President Johnson, but I'd love to come up."

The conversation ended on a reasonably tranquil note with the understanding that I would come to visit.

I immediately called the head of our largest advertiser, the Joske's department store, and asked if he would be interested in taking page three of our next day's paper, a prime spot reserved regularly for Joske ads, to run an ad with a "Get Well, President Johnson" message. Recognizing it would be great PR, the Joske president, Pat Segner, agreed without hesitation.

The beautifully prepared ad with a page-dominating photo of LBJ taken at the peak of his power appeared on page three the next day with the "Get Well, President Johnson" message. I had our art department prepare a glossy copy of the ad and headed for Brooke Army Medical Center. LBJ was clearly touched by the gesture, and demonstrated the soft and appealing side of his personality only those close to him saw with any regularity.

To be very clear, I certainly was not an intimate of LBJ. I was, however, privileged to have a few ringside seats at the Johnson show. I was in his company during the 1972 presidential election when he was urged by many in his party to weigh in with criticism about Nixon's actions. He replied on the record that we should have "one president at a time."

On the day he died, January 22, 1973, President Johnson dictated a letter to me that he never got the chance to sign. He had written me to acknowledge my letter to Walter W. Heller, chairman of the Council of Economic Advisors during the Kennedy and Johnson administrations, a copy of which I had sent to President Johnson. Dr. Heller had come to San Antonio at my invitation to give a speech at an economic forum being sponsored, I believe, by the Chamber of Commerce. Heller had tied in a visit with the Johnsons as part of his trip, and the LBJ letter described glowingly the day he showed Heller around.

President Johnson's secretary, Mary Rather, had the presence of mind to send the unsigned letter to me accompanied by her own letter, which read: "President Johnson did not have the opportunity to sign his mail on January 22 but he had dictated this letter to you and we transcribed it thinking you might like to have it." Both letters hang on my office wall alongside a framed version of the editorial I had written, published in our paper on January 23, saying goodbye to LBJ.

A few days later I drove to Stonewall to be a spectator at his inspiring burial service, conducted in a small family cemetery on the LBJ Ranch. As I recall it, John Connally, Billy Graham, and Barbara Jordan, among others, gave powerful eulogies.

◆

I learned that Richard Milhous Nixon had died when I read the announcement of his death on April 23, 1994, by Jonathan Weil, a spokesman for New York Hospital, of which I was vice chairman at the time. I had, naturally, been following the announcements of his condition by Dr. Fred Plum, the patrician chief of neurology at Cornell and the hospital.

As a newspaper publisher and an officer in various newspaper associations I attended several formal briefings. I heard President Nixon make his case for the price controls he implemented during his first term, the Vietnam War, the end of the gold standard, and all manner of presidential initiatives. The Nixon encounter that impressed me mightily was much closer to home.

At a reception at John Connally's ranch, I discovered a relaxed and chatty Nixon. He wore a powder blue blazer and smiled broadly as he talked to the guests, not at all the Nixon I had read about and seen on television. No sign of the "You won't have Nixon to kick around anymore."

When Luella and I approached him in the receiving line, I explained that we were meeting in the home of my cousin John Connally. He went to great lengths to describe his enormous respect for Connally. He referred to him as first among cabinet members and predicted he would one day sit in the Oval Office.

Later it was pretty common knowledge, and I believe it to be the case, that when Spiro Agnew was forced to resign Nixon wanted to appoint Connally as vice president instead of Gerald Ford. He was restrained because of impending charges against Connally related to a so-called bribe by milk producers. Connally was acquitted by a D.C. jury of what clearly were trumped-up charges. At the trial the jury heard first ladies Jacqueline Kennedy and Lady Bird Johnson, Billy Graham, Dean Rusk, and Barbara Jordan attest to Connally's good character. I've often thought about how close Nixon came to giving our family a relative in the White House.

During what turned out to be the final days of the Nixon administration at another presidential briefing, I was stunned to see how bad Nixon looked and how nonlinear his presentation was. I always believed that two world leaders, Margaret Thatcher and

Richard Nixon, were the most skilled I ever heard at verbally depicting the entire world, the good and bad guys, the prognosis for peace or war. Not that night.

Nixon entered my life again in 1986, when the American Newspaper Publishers Association held its annual convention in San Francisco. A highlight of the annual gathering in those days was the Associated Press luncheon. The AP almost always came up with a speaker of note. Presumably having decided that the standoff between the press and Richard Nixon had to end sometime, the AP invited Nixon to deliver the coveted luncheon speech.

He wowed this audience of negatively predisposed newspaper executives in a way no one could have predicted. For virtually a full hour, as I recall it, he described the world with conviction and powerful oratory nobody there would soon forget. This, twelve years after he gave the classic Nixon wave as he walked into Marine One for the last time.

At the cocktail reception preceding the luncheon, I approached Nixon just as he was reaching out to shake the hand of Katharine Graham of the *Washington Post*, their first face-to-face encounter since the *Post* had played a major role in bringing down his presidency. The AP picture that ran in newspapers all over the country captured that historic moment: Nixon and Kay shaking hands with shit-eating grins on their faces. Through their outstretched arms one could clearly see me. I have copies of that picture in my office, at home, and in my picture file. Witness to history.

Some years later, I was attending a board meeting of Chemical Bank and I started to experience chest pains. After toughing it out for a few minutes I wasn't feeling any better. The pains were severe enough that I concluded I must be having a heart attack.

I advised the chairman, John McGillicuddy, what I thought was happening and that I had to leave. I slipped out of the boardroom, called Harvey Klein, my doctor, and told him I was bringing him a heart attack.

My driver had left, not expecting me to come out for hours, so I jumped into a cab. I made the mistake of telling the cabbie about my problem, and at breakneck speed he damned near killed us both on the way to New York Hospital.

As I entered the lobby of the hospital's Starr Pavilion, where my doctor's office was then located, I observed a fair amount of commotion off to my right, away from the elevators. I spotted Richard Nixon in the middle of the crowd. By the time I got an elevator up to Dr. Klein's office, guess who had arrived? Richard Nixon. I thought: I'm a goner. I'm having a heart attack, and Dr. Klein is going to feel obligated to take care of Nixon first.

Hope returned. Dr. Klein, holding Nixon by the arm, brought him over to me. "Frank, you know President Nixon, don't you?"

"I do, Harvey. Among the times President Nixon and I have connected was when Arbor House, then owned by Hearst, was publishing one of his books."

(I'm thinking: "Harvey, get me out of here. I'm having a heart attack!")

Dr. Klein turns Nixon's arm loose and grabs mine as if to lead me away to whatever treatment he was going to administer.

"You know, Frank, I have many connections to your company," Nixon says, arm outstretched, holding us back from leaving, "I knew Dick Berlin," he continued. "And in addition to other connections with your group I have a friend who distributes your magazines in New Jersey and he says they're great sellers."

(I'm thinking: "I'm going to stand right here, good guy that I am, and get killed by Richard Nixon.")

Finally, Dr. Klein was able to pull me away, "Excuse us, President Nixon, I have to give Mr. Bennack some important tests."

Long story short: I had a case of pericarditis, a condition where the sack around the heart is inflamed and the patient can feel like he/she is having a heart attack. It can be dangerous. Mine wasn't. Dr. Klein brought me back to full health, leaving us both with a story we have told a hundred times.

◆

President Gerald Ford had visited us at Hearst's Eighth Avenue headquarters when he was vice president and impressed us with his down-to-earth and practical view of the world. I saw him again after the Nixon resignation. He knew the pardon had put him in political jeopardy, but he had a country to run while moving it toward the healing we all wished for.

When Nixon was called on to appoint someone to succeed the disgraced Agnew, it was thought that since that appointee was not elected, he should be someone who did not aspire to the presidency—just someone to serve the nation in the interim.

But I recall a one-liner Ford got off as the Republican speaker at the Gridiron Club's white-tie dinner. The Gridiron is one of Washington's unique events: members of the press roast the political establishment, and the politicos return the favor. Ford, in his speech for the Republicans, said something like: "After a party the other night, Betty and I were being driven to the vice president's residence, and we passed the White House. I said, 'You know, Betty, if we lived there, we'd be home now.'"

We had no doubt that if he ascended to the presidency he would want to run for reelection.

◆

The first national political convention I ever attended was the 1976 Democratic Convention held in New York City. By then John Miller had named me executive vice president, and I was anxious to join our journalists covering the convention. I went to several events, including the night when Jimmy Carter was nominated. I thought his speech and the nominating ceremony were glorious.

We invited the nominee to come to Hearst headquarters and meet with our newspaper and magazine editors and as many writers and reporters as we could assemble on short notice. John Miller and the other senior corporate officers would usually join a session like this, and they did that day.

The invitation had been extended in my name and it would be my show. Along with being more nervous than usual, I was somewhat apprehensive that Carter might call me out because I had recruited a known Carter detractor, Reg Murphy, as editor and publisher of our *San Francisco Examiner*. Murphy had been editor of the *Atlanta Constitution* and *Journal*, and had, at least in Carter's mind, given the prospective nominee and Georgia governor a hard time. Among other shots across the bow, Murphy was said to have authored the headline "JIMMY CARTER IS RUNNING FOR WHAT?" when Carter had indicated he was making a presidential run.

Carter was brilliant that day. Clearly at the top of his game, he looked and sounded presidential. His opening remarks were persuasive, his responses to questions flawless. Everyone was impressed and convinced a new political star had been born.

I kept thinking the Reg Murphy issue would come up at any time.

Carter's handlers, as is always the case with political figures, finally whispered he had to go. The session ended on a high note: Jimmy Carter had every intention of becoming president of the United States, and he was sure we and our readers would be delighted that was the case.

Everybody stayed in place while I walked Carter and his entourage to the elevator. The elevator doors opened, the candidate stepped in, turned around, stuck out his arms at shoulder height and held the elevator doors open with both hands.

"Frank, I know it must be my fault, but I sure would like to know what I did to anger Reg Murphy; I'm sure it was my fault," he said at a level just above a whisper. He dropped his arms, and the elevator doors closed, and Jimmy Carter went on to become the thirty-ninth president of the United States.

Although I never spoke to him about the subject before he took the action, in 1979 President Carter commuted Patty Hearst's prison sentence but did not pardon her as we hoped he would. (Bill Clinton, with Carter's urging, did grant her a full pardon in 2001.) Almost every time I saw President Carter after that he asked about Patty and her family.

In 2013, former president Carter made a return visit to Hearst headquarters to talk about the Carter Center and its Global Development Initiative. I pulled out the picture of the two of us taken thirty-seven years earlier, and we posed for a 2013 version.

We each signed both the 1976 and 2013 pictures. Remarkably he seemed to want copies as much as I did.

President Carter and I met numerous times, admittedly mostly after he left the presidency. He agreed to give a speech at a charity fundraiser I was involved in and even flew to California to address a Magazine Publishers Association gathering at my request. He occasionally called when he was in New York, once inviting me to breakfast with him and Rosalynn. Several years ago, I met the former president and Mrs. Carter in Beijing where, unrelated to us, one of our Chinese partners had provided office space for the Carter Initiative.

As someone writing his first book, I am reminded of an exchange with the former president that brought then, and brings now, a broad smile to my face. A rather distressed-looking Jimmy Carter, during one of our meetings, apropos of nothing, said, "Frank, let me give you some advice. Don't ever write a book with your wife." It was clear the book he and Mrs. Carter had done together had been a genuine trial. He didn't say it, but knowing Jimmy Carter's moral compass, I could almost imagine he was thinking about the waggish remark: Divorce, never. Murder, maybe!

He has been kind enough to follow my career, and on one occasion said: "I'm proud of you, Frank." Well, I'm proud of Jimmy Carter and my relationship with him.

◆

Ronald Reagan had a relatively close association with Hearst well before I came on the scene. Like many Hollywood types he knew some of Mr. Hearst's sons. He definitely knew grandson George and granddaughter Phoebe, and likely knew the founder. As governor he appointed Catherine Hearst, Randolph Hearst's wife, to the University of California Board of Regents.

I met him a few times while he was governor, but the most extensive visit I ever had with him was in the 1970s, backstage at a convention of the American Newspaper Publishers Association. Our King Features Syndicate was representing Reagan in the distribution of his column to newspapers across the country, and he and his media representative had shown up at the convention to promote the column. Curiously, the individual representing him in both his newspaper column and the radio show that Reagan syndicated after his stint as governor was Harry O'Conner—the "Mushmouth Harry O'Conner" I knew as a disk jockey in San Antonio during my stint as a teenage DJ.

We were in the greenroom for quite a long period of time that day, and after a far-reaching and thoroughly relaxed conversation I felt I knew the real Ronald Reagan.

I don't think I saw Reagan again until he was on the presidential campaign trail. While running for his first term in 1980, he made the obligatory stops in New York, despite the general opinion that a Republican couldn't win the state. Of course, New York was among the forty-four states he did win.

Reagan and his campaign entourage—Pat Buchanan, William Casey, and James Brady, among others—came for lunch in the *Good Housekeeping* dining room, where other presidents and presidential candidates had also dined. My favorite picture with a president, in this case a president-to-be, was taken that day. Reagan, never caught without something clever to say, had asked me

to grant him the *Good Housekeeping* "Seal of Approval." He said
he thought it might help in his campaign. I explained that, despite
my being president and CEO of Hearst, I did not have the power
to grant the Seal. Only the editor of *Good Housekeeping* had that
power. Further, the warranty for which the Seal was famous stipu-
lated that if the product bearing the Seal "proved to be defective
within four years," *Good Housekeeping* would refund the consum-
er's money.

Apparently, the symmetry of the four years with the presidential term and the idea of a "defective" president hit a funny bone,
and Reagan laughed robustly. The picture I love has me making
the explanation with a serious expression on my face and him
breaking up.

◆

George Herbert Walker Bush was a congressman from Houston
in 1970 when I was introduced to him by Henry B. González, the
illustrious congressman representing the Texas 20th Congressional
district. As publisher of the *San Antonio Light*, I was hawking the
merits of the Newspaper Preservation Act, which all but one member of the Texas congressional delegation ultimately voted for.

Bush came into sharper focus for me when he decided to run
for the United States Senate. Newspaper publishers have no shortage of opportunities to meet such candidates for statewide office,
so I got even better acquainted with him during the two runs he
made for the Senate. In 1964, at a time when Texas was not yet pre-
dictably Republican, Bush got 43.56 percent of the vote in a loss
to incumbent Democratic senator Ralph Yarborough. In 1970 he
took another run at the office. Lloyd Bentsen had defeated Yarbor-

ough in the Democratic primary and Bush, who, I'm quite sure, felt he could defeat Yarborough in the general election, ended up running against the popular Bentsen, who had backing from LBJ, John Connally, and the strong conservative Democratic establishment. Bush got 46.45 percent of the vote, an excellent showing against a powerful opponent.

That election resulted in the loss, at least temporarily, of a casual friendship I felt I had established with Bush. Not only did our paper endorse Bentsen in the general election, I believe we were the first major Texas paper to do so. Through our reporters covering the race I heard that my old congressman friend was not only disappointed but also surprised. Actually, he was pissed.

George Bush's 1971–1973 stint as ambassador to the U.N., his 1974 role as envoy to China, and his 1976 appointment as director of the CIA not only prepared him for his future roles as vice president and president but apparently washed away all memories of earlier political slights. Every encounter I had with him after that was warm. On the final day of his successful 1988 presidential campaign he visited my associates and me at our New York headquarters. His confidence in the election outcome was palpable.

Our relationship had been further enhanced when we acquired the *Houston Chronicle* in 1987 because of a close personal relationship Bush had with our publisher there, Richard J. V. Johnson.

When I was president of ANPA, the American Newspaper Publishers Association (later named Newspaper Association of America, and now News Media Alliance), I received a framed picture from President Bush on the occasion of my sixtieth birthday in January 1993—he had been defeated by Bill Clinton but was still in the Oval Office—accompanied by a letter that said, in part,

"You are Number One at the American Newspaper Association and Number One in the hearts of the Hearst Corporation. When I was 60 I was still Number Two, which means that everything up until 60 is preparation and the best is yet to come."

One of my most memorable days with any president came when George H. W. Bush invited me to participate in a leadership conference at Texas A&M, the site of his presidential library. Before a large auditorium filled with students, the former president questioned his pals Chuck Norris and Robert Mosbacher, who had served as the former president's secretary of commerce, daughter-in-law Laura Bush, and me on the key elements of leadership. Luella and I spent the entire day there with the Bushes, visiting the full-size model of the president's quarters on Air Force One and the rest of the presidential library while participating in hours of fascinating conversation about the presidency.

To my regret I was unable to accept the Bush family's invitation to attend Barbara Bush's funeral in April 2018. I had my own moment of silence remembering how much I enjoyed our visit with her at the presidential library and our pleasure in 1990 when we published her bestseller, *Millie's Book*, the proceeds of which went to her literacy charity.

Two thousand eighteen was a difficult year for the Bush family, ending with a respectful and tearful goodbye to George Herbert Walker Bush. I was privileged to attend the tribute to his life at the Washington National Cathedral on December 5, 2018. The nation's response, and the response of those who spoke so eloquently there and in the other ceremonies over the several days of mourning, was remarkably clear and consistent. Despite the failure to reelect him to a second term, Americans judge the Bush administration to have been among the most consequential in modern times and judge George H. W. Bush as a patriot, public servant, and role model of uncommon stature. I personally value the almost fifty years I knew him and admire not only what he achieved but who he was.

◆

Bill Clinton was a relatively new incumbent when he made an appearance at the annual convention of the Newspaper Association of America in Boston. I got my introduction to this self-confident and vigorous new president when I drew the assignment of moderating a Q&A before the assembled newspaper industry brass. Everything started as expected. I did the introduction and opened the proceedings to audience questions. After calling on one or two questioners, it became obvious that my role had become superfluous—Clinton began to call on the questioners himself. I remember thinking as I stood on the stage like the proverbial potted palm, that if there was any doubt about this new president's ability to take charge, that question had been answered.

Anybody in any sort of leadership in New York after the Clinton presidency has likely had ample contact with William Jefferson Clinton. I've attended his annual gathering of the Clinton Global Initiative a time or two, and he has visited us at Hearst headquarters a number of times. He's always open to a discussion of the world around him. Importantly, I shared the platform with him for the dedication of the new Milstein Family Heart Center at the Columbia campus of NewYork-Presbyterian Hospital. The care and treatment he received from Columbia doctors left him enormously grateful and ready to help that institution any way he can.

◆

George W. Bush was too young and not so much in the public eye for me to have known him when I was publisher in San Antonio, and our paths didn't cross until he was governor of Texas. My first meeting with him occurred when George Irish, then the president of our newspapers, who got to know Bush well during Irish's tour as publisher of our *Midland Reporter Telegram*, got Bush to agree to a meeting with the Hearst newspaper editors at the Governor's Mansion in Austin. I had an opportunity to talk with him about my long association with his father. As everyone knows, he is charming and easy to talk to.

Years later, again through George Irish, Mary Lake and I, along with Vic Ganzi, who was CEO of Hearst at the time, Ganzi's wife, Pat, and George and his wife, Jeanie, were invited to visit President Bush in the Oval Office. The Iraq War was at the top of everyone's mind at the time, and Bush gave a spirited defense of it between efforts on my part to lighten the visit by talking about our respective Texas ranches. Although polite and welcoming, Bush was understandably in no mood that day for small talk.

There was another interesting sidenote that day. As a high school senior, Karl Rove, the future Republican political consultant who became senior advisor and deputy chief of staff during the George W. Bush administration, had been a delegate in the Hearst Foundations' Senate Youth Program. Along with awarding scholarship money, that program takes one-hundred-plus students to Washington for a weeklong experience of a lifetime. Rove, who credits the program as being important to his getting a college education and entering public life, stood by in the Oval

Office and chatted with us after our presidential visit. He thoroughly charmed the women in our group, a reaction they hadn't anticipated but which came as no surprise to me.

In 2002 Marianne Means, a White House correspondent, reporter, and columnist in the Hearst Washington Bureau who had gained national stature covering the administrations of both Presidents Kennedy and Johnson, served as president of the Gridiron Club. At the annual dinner, the CEO of the club president's company is seated next to the president on the dais.

I have been known to suggest that the Gridiron evening "goes on longer than World War II"—in point of fact it can last four hours or more. That produced the opportunity for me to have the longest and most comprehensive conversation I ever had with George W. Bush up until that time. The discussion was far-ranging and covered everything from our respective Texas histories to the state of the world. What I recall especially was that I described for President Bush my first experience of the Gridiron, twenty or twenty-five years earlier: The Marine Band played all of the armed service anthems. By tradition, those of us who had served stood when the anthem for our branch of service was played. In those days a sizable percentage of those in attendance would be standing. By 2002 things were very different: a few standing here, another few standing there, a fraction of the veterans in days gone by. President Bush said, "Then I guess my job is to be sure the smallest number possible in the future are standing."

In April 2016, both the former president and first lady Laura Bush accepted our invitation to attend an offsite business retreat of Hearst executives and spouses. They subjected themselves to my no-holds-barred interview. We found his answers enlightening, relaxed, and candid. Mrs. Bush's answers were, as always, frank and to the point. I think the former first couple enjoyed it as much as we did.

◆

In July 2009, during my tenure as chairman of Lincoln Center for the Performing Arts, President Barack Obama attended a memorial service held at the center for Walter Cronkite, who along with Edward R. Murrow was television's most esteemed news anchor ever. Katherine Farley, who would succeed me as chair, and her husband, Jerry Speyer, Lincoln Center president Reynold Levy and his wife, Liz, and Mary Lake and I were granted a brief private meeting prior to the memorial. It was the first time I had met President Obama since he had taken office six months earlier. He was unhurried, knowledgeable about both Lincoln Center and about Cronkite, whom I had gotten to know pretty well as a result of his engagement with The Museum of Television & Radio. The freshman chief executive was clearly presidential. We were honored to meet our first African American commander-in-chief.

Good fortune had it that Chuck Lewis, the longtime chief of the Washington Bureau of the Hearst Newspapers, was the 2013 president of the Gridiron Club. Thus, I got a second chance to spend three or four hours on the dais next to a president, this time Barack Obama. The evening seemed to go faster than usual, and I found the president open, accessible, even chatty. As with President Bush in my earlier Gridiron opportunity, the conversation ranged from matters of minor interest to major.

He expressed concern about the current plight of newspapers, and asked a very thoughtful question: "If your newspapers just broke even, would you still publish them?" I replied that Hearst, for reasons related to our history and DNA, and importantly because of profitable businesses we have in television, cable, magazines, databases, and more, undoubtedly would. I added, however, that publishers who don't have our financial strength and who rely on newspaper profits to attract and justify capital investment, would, unhappily, probably have to give a different answer. He acknowledged that was the concern implied in his question.

Only a short time after the Gridiron experience I visited the White House with that year's high school senior delegates to the Hearst Senate Youth week. As is typical, the hundred-plus students are lined up in the center of the room on risers, seven or eight rows deep, waiting to be addressed by the president. The directors of the sponsoring Hearst Foundations and Foundation employees are seated inconspicuously at the side of the room.

President Obama began his remarks by praising the young people for their leadership and accomplishments. He said that their generation is in many respects better educated, better informed, and more impressive than older generations, including his. He did believe, he said, that there was one concerning characteristic. Their generation was inclined to expect that they should get to the top without stepping on every rung of the ladder on the way up. He followed with something like, "Take old Frank over there. He started at the very bottom, as a classified ad salesman, and worked his way up, a step at a time, to be the head of the huge organization that made this program possible."

The president of the United States was telling, in summary, my life story, all of which he could have only remembered from

our visit at the Gridiron Dinner. Or did he have splendid staffing? In 2018, when I got the opportunity to speak to Mrs. Obama on the occasion of previewing her book, *Becoming*, I told her what her husband had said was, perhaps, the most flattering and humbling thing ever said about me by a president of the United States. She said, "He just remembered what you had told him."

◆

Shortly after I moved to New York, John Miller introduced me to the charity United Cerebral Palsy and the civic leaders who founded it. Not only had John made it a favorite charity of our Company so, too, had his predecessors, Dick Berlin and Frank Massi. My involvement in UCP was accelerated when I succeeded John as CEO in 1979. It was through UCP that I met Donald Trump.

Fred Trump, a successful real estate developer and Donald's father, had taken an interest in the charity at the urging of UCP founders Leonard Goldenson and Jack Hausman. Later, Donald stepped up in support of UCP. More than once, Donald and Ivana and Luella and I co-chaired events for UCP. One that I remember particularly that kept us up late was a "virgin" gambling event; attendees bid on swag that had been donated for the occasion using chips bought with their money. The money, of course, went to the charity. After the "gambling" concluded, we all stayed around for a celebratory breakfast and talked about how much had been raised for UCP. My Hearst associates loved this event above all the other charitable galas we supported, and we enjoyed the time spent with the Trumps.

Leonard Goldenson, encouraged by his cofounder Jack Hausman, recruited Bob Hope, Dennis James, and other celebrities to

the UCP cause. Hausman did his fundraising on the golf course at Deepdale, an exclusive Long Island club. Jack would call and tell you he had Bob Hope and, sometimes, Donald Trump coming for a game of golf, and urge you to join. I did, more than once.

In 2017 I again accompanied the Hearst Senate Youth students on their visit to the White House. After his remarks to the assembled students, President Trump came over to visit briefly with the Foundation directors and the military and civilian chaperones. My fellow foundation director, David Barrett, said something to the effect of "Mr. President, there's somebody you've known a long time over here." The president hurried over, grabbed me by the arm, and spun us around to face the students. He described how we had known each other for forty years and said some terribly flattering things about me, along with asking Will Hearst, who stood alongside me, if he knew "how lucky the Hearst family had been to have had me running the company."

◆

I've written at some length about the presidents I've "known." You have surely recognized that I was not, and do not, qualify as an intimate of any of them. My professional role has always dictated that I've never served on any electoral campaign committee or been active in any political party. I've never even made a political contribution for fear of sending an inadvertent signal of bias or candidate preference to those in our organization who cover government and politics. My purpose in including this element in the book is to underline the privilege this former classified advertising salesman from San Antonio has enjoyed solely by virtue of

the role with which I have been entrusted in this great Company. I also unabashedly respect the office of the president of the United States. While I accept the American credo that all of the incumbents were born equal, like everyone else I recognize their contributions to the nation are not.

CHAPTER 16

Flunking Retirement

Thanks to a terrific team and a supportive board, in my first twenty-three years as CEO, revenues of the Company had grown more than sevenfold and income had increased more than fourteen times. In the most recent five years, 1996 through 2001, we did even better—Hearst revenue grew 50 percent and earnings grew 89 percent. Importantly, all of us felt that we had a good trajectory going forward.

In 2002 I would reach sixty-nine years of age. I didn't feel my contribution was complete, but I also didn't want to be seen as holding on too long. Besides, in our culture, where our most senior leadership serves as lifetime trustees of the Hearst Family Trust, it was clear that I could continue to be engaged and influence the Company's direction even if I stepped aside as CEO.

Gil Maurer had agreed that Victor Ganzi was the logical successor. Vic had succeeded Gil as chief operating officer, a role he clearly saw as CEO-in-training; he wouldn't be wrong to seek his fortunes elsewhere if I signed a new multiyear contract as Hearst CEO. I decided to ask the board to approve my move to the dual role of vice chairman and chairman of the Executive Committee.

It did. When I retired from the CEO position in June of 2002, Vic Ganzi was elected president and chief executive officer.

About Vic: In the late 1980s, Harvey Lipton, for decades the general counsel of Hearst, spoke to me about his desire to retire from that post and serve out the rest of his tenure as a trustee. We discussed potential successors; we both thought that Vic Ganzi, managing partner at the law firm Rogers & Wells, with whom we had worked on a number of transactions, was an especially attractive candidate. We also thought that as he had both accounting and law degrees and was clearly very smart he would bring more than his special expertise as a tax lawyer to Hearst.

An episode years later reveals how smart. The Hearst Board had elected Vic Ganzi to succeed me, but I was still CEO when Vic and I made a joint appearance at a gathering of our broadcast managers. In his introduction of Vic, with me plainly standing beside him with my bare face hanging out, David Barrett—foundation director, former head of Hearst Broadcasting, and a trustee—loudly intoned, "Our new president, Vic Ganzi, is definitely the smartest man I ever met." I responded in the way I've read that George Bernard Shaw responded to all personal comments, positive or negative: "You may be right." This moment still is good for a red-faced smile from David Barrett whenever I remind him about it.

Both Lipton and I had previously engaged in informal exploratory discussions with Vic. He told us that he had assured Rogers & Wells's eminent partner, former secretary of state William P. Rogers, that he would stay at the law firm for a certain number of years. After that, he said, he was free to consider a move. In 1990, when he was forty-three years old, we brought him on board as general counsel. In 1992, we named him chief financial and legal officer. In 1997, we elected him executive vice president, and a year after that added the title of chief operating officer upon Gil Maurer's retirement from that position. And then the step up to CEO.

◆

In 2002 Hearst had a new CEO, and I had a life that was certain to be different from the twenty-three years I had been CEO and the fifty-two years I had spent doing a full day's work. Someone had told me what I had long suspected—"If you like Saturday, you'll like retirement"—so I quickly expanded my pro bono life, spending more time as vice chairman of NewYork-Presbyterian Hospital and chairman of The Museum of Television & Radio.

But it didn't feel like I was working less hard for Hearst, as I advised and supported Vic as he undertook to keep the Company growing. In 2004, we acquired Zynx Health, station WMTW-TV in Portland, Maine, and made the initial 20 percent investment in the ratings agency and financial services company Fitch. In 2006, we purchased a 31 percent stake in MediaNews Group and acquired Orlando station WXCF-TV. The next year we added the Danbury *News-Times*, the Stamford *Advocate*, and *Greenwich Time*. There were also a number of additions to our U.K. subsidiary and the process of launching new magazine titles in the United States and abroad continued.

When my wife passed away, less than a year after I stepped down from the CEO position, Vic Ganzi and his wife, Patricia, gave me a great deal of attention and moral support, for which I will always be grateful. Many a night they bought me dinner at the Palm, of which Vic's family is an owner, and often made the hours when I wasn't working more bearable.

What changed most for me, particularly after Mary Lake and I were married in 2005, was personal travel. It would be impossible to calculate how many days of earned vacation time I had left unused over a fifty-plus-year stretch in Hearst management. I don't raise that because I felt shortchanged; to the contrary, I loved what I did for a living and seldom enjoyed being away from the job for periods greater than a week or so. Now I could still live up to my obligations to Hearst—and spend two weeks in Vietnam and Bhutan. I could travel to Asmara and beyond to assist Mary Lake in the Eritrea Women's Project she started to rescue hundreds of women in that Horn of Africa country from the horrors of fistulas resulting from traumatic births. One July we rented a villa in Tuscany and stayed for an entire month while family members plus Gil and Ann Maurer, Vic and Pat Ganzi, and other friends and business associates visited us. A major bonus: Our children, who were a part of most of our travels during those six years, learned that the world has much to offer in the way of education, natural and man-made beauty, and the understanding that what we know is not all there is to know. They now travel whenever and wherever they can.

Near the end of those six years, in February 2008, Mary Lake and I accompanied the New York Philharmonic orchestra to Pyongyang, North Korea, where their concert represented a significant event in North Korea's relations with the United States. I was then chairman of Lincoln Center, and we all had high hopes that such a cultural exchange would lead to more.

That Pyongyang trip was a mixture of emotionally rewarding and challenging experiences. Philharmonic conductor Lorin Maazel orchestrated a brilliant program that opened with both national anthems—with North Korea's performed first, followed by "The Star-Spangled Banner." Maazel's selections included Antonín Dvořák's Symphony No. 9, "From the New World," and Gershwin's *An American in Paris*, followed by the performance of the Korean folk song "Arirang." Originating in Gangwon Province six hundred years ago, "Arirang" is a musical masterpiece associated with romantic sorrow, separation, and reunion. It had been the anthem of resistance during the 1910–1945 occupation of Korea by Imperial Japan. According to Reuters, this night in Pyongyang the crowd of mostly communist elite middle-age men in dark suits "gave the performance a standing ovation. Some of the musicians were so overcome they left the stage in tears." We were sure the powerful experience had invoked deep feelings in the audience and thoughts of divided Koreas, and Korean families, irrevocably separated.

We could not have been better treated throughout our stay. We were welcomed to North Korea's libraries; Mary Lake and I visited a hospital's maternity ward; others went to cultural or educational centers. Of course our cell phones had been taken from us on arrival and returned when we departed.

One episode caused a bit of tension. We were driven by bus to a memorial honoring the Great Leader and founder, the late Kim Il Sung. Awaiting our arrival were beautifully dressed women with flower arrangements and floral wreaths they had apparently hoped we would lay at the foot of the memorial. Everyone on the bus had the same thought: This would be a propaganda photo of Americans paying homage to the Great Leader. We stayed in our seats. Eventually the bus doors closed, and we drove on to the next destination.

◆

I was having fun. And time truly did fly by. Then, on June 18, 2008—six years after I stepped out of the CEO chair—Vic Ganzi resigned. The Hearst press release said it best: "The reason for his resignation was irreconcilable policy differences with the Board of Trustees about the future direction of the Company. Victor Ganzi worked diligently to direct Hearst during a critical time, and we are appreciative of his commitment to Hearst's success. We wish him well in his future endeavors." And Vic went on to score many notable achievements following his eighteen years at Hearst.

When I took on the Lincoln Center chairmanship, Mary Lake gave her full support. She gave it again when I was asked to return to the CEO role at Hearst. She understood what I did: It would be only until we could decide on new leadership. We thought that meant about a year. As it turned out, the Great Recession had begun the previous December; on September 15, 2008, three months after I had again become CEO, Lehman Brothers declared bankruptcy. Reality changed overnight. Hearst, like every other company, needed an experienced and steady hand. The board thought that might be me. And that is how I came to be CEO for five more years.

Those five years, June 2008 to June 2013, are known at Hearst as "Bennack 2.0." And as fate would have it, those five years may have been the best years of this flunked-retiree-turned-CEO's twenty-eight years as CEO. They were also among the very best for Hearst. We saw a decline in revenue and earnings only in one year, 2008. Every year after that was an up year. By 2013, revenue and earnings had risen 30 percent and 40 percent, respectively, above the pre-recession all-time highs. We routinely compare our performance with those of our public competitors; and our recovery from the 2008 trough to 2013 was, if not the best of any of them, better than most. Importantly, through internal promotions and some strategic recruiting, we put a new management team in place. In June of 2013, Steve Swartz succeeded me as CEO.

Steven R. Swartz graduated from Harvard in 1984 and began his career as a reporter for the *Wall Street Journal*. In 1989 he was tapped as an editor on the *Journal*'s Page One staff. In 1991, the *Journal*'s editor, Norman Pearlstine, who later served with great distinction at Time, Inc., Bloomberg, and the *Los Angeles Times*, named Steve as founding editor of *SmartMoney*, a joint venture publication we at Hearst launched with Dow Jones. During Steve's time there *SmartMoney* won two National Magazine Awards and was named *Advertising Age*'s Magazine of the Year.

From day one, Gil Maurer and I knew this was a guy who would vault up the ladder someplace, and we'd be well advised to ensure that it would be with us. In 2000 we lured him away from *SmartMoney* to become the deputy head of our newspaper group. In December 2008, five months after I returned as CEO, we appointed him president of Hearst Newspapers. He courageously laid the groundwork for two new newspaper requirements: In an era of declining ad revenues the reader needs to share more of the cost of a newspaper, and newspapers must show digital growth. It was a winning strategy, brilliantly executed: Our papers have seen better-than-average performance ever since. In 2011, as I started to think about when I should step down for the second time, I asked the board to name Steve our chief operating officer, where he made an even greater contribution.

So what happened during Bennack 2.0? We launched *Food Network* and *HGTV* magazines, with notable success. We acquired MCG Health, one of our most successful database businesses, and we increased our position in Fitch from 20 percent to 50 percent, and laid the groundwork for owning the entire company, which happened on Steve's watch in 2018. We bought out all the stock we didn't own in Hearst-Argyle, the broadcast company we had taken public in 1998. We acquired and integrated into Hearst the nearly one hundred magazines—including such important titles as *ELLE, ELLE DECOR, Woman's Day*, and *Car and Driver*—in fourteen countries owned by Lagardère. With our partners, The Walt Disney Company, we purchased the 25 percent of A&E and The History Channel that had been owned by NBC. We accelerated the development of digital at our newspapers, magazines, TV stations, and Business Media units. And we set the stage and built the team for the full realization of a digital transition that Steve Swartz and his team are achieving.

When I stepped down from the CEO position the second time, there was no question: I had flunked retirement, succeeded in the makeup course, and had now officially graduated. The board generously rewarded me by adding executive to my prior title as vice chairman. As executive vice chairman, I am advising and supporting Steve Swartz and our senior team whenever and wherever they need it. That need will be less and less as time goes along. I've also retained chairmanship of Hearst's Executive and Finance Committees, and of our U.K. subsidiary.

Seldom does anyone refer to me as retired.

CHAPTER 17

Maybe the Best Thing Four Businessmen Ever Did: Merge The New York and Presbyterian Hospitals

The nonprofit institution with which I have the longest affiliation—and arguably the institution with which I have been associated that does the greatest good for the city, the nation, and even the world—is NewYork-Presbyterian Hospital.

I joined the board of what was then The New York Hospital in 1979. Just shy of a decade later, in my capacity as vice chairman I participated, with three enlightened civic leaders and two inspired physician-administrators, in a merger of The New York Hospital and Columbia Presbyterian, New York City's largest and most consequential academic hospitals. That merger reshaped the health care landscape in the New York region. Because of the importance of the two institutions, that merger may extend beyond New York as among the most important in modern hospital history.

As is often the case in New York, the civic leaders were CEOs: John McGillicuddy, retired chairman and CEO of Chemical Bank (previously Manufacturers Hanover), Dan Burke, former president and CEO of Capital Cities/ABC, John Mack, president of Morgan Stanley, and me. The four of us negotiated the merger with the help of two doctors, David B. Skinner and William T. Speck. Much was at stake, for this was a merger of necessity; medical care had dramatically changed in America, and each of the institutions had experienced recent annual losses of as much as $50 million.

The New York Hospital had been founded in 1771 with a charter from England's King George III, and is the third oldest hospital in the United States. Its history includes Alexander Hamilton, who never studied nor practiced medicine, but as a Founding Father was among the leaders of the day in establishing the country's first hospitals—as was Aaron Burr, who would fatally shoot him in a duel. According to research done by the hospital, both men were among those who "deserve credit for laying the nascent Republic's health care foundation." Legend has it that Hamilton stood on the steps of King's College in an effort to disband an angry mob accusing the medical students of grave robbing. Since 1898 The New York Hospital has been associated with what is today known as Weill Cornell Medical College.

The Presbyterian Hospital was founded in 1868, and was associated with Columbia University College of Physicians and Surgeons, which has been around since 1767 as the medical department of King's College, predecessor to Columbia.

There were two large challenges to the merger. The first: The newly created single hospital would be the first ever to have affiliation with two world-class medical schools and universities. The second was more personal: Maurice "Hank" Greenberg at New York Hospital and Seymour Milstein at Presbyterian—each institution's most influential and generous "patriarch"—expressed grave reservations bordering on opposition. Happily, Greenberg and Milstein continued to provide indispensable guidance and financial support to the merged hospital, as has the family of Milstein, who died in 2001. It would be hard to imagine that anyone could have been more significant in the long history of the legacy of New York Hospital, Columbia Presbyterian Hospital, and the successor NewYork-Presbyterian Hospital than Greenberg and Milstein.

Both boards concluded that joining forces was the wisest course of action in an environment of changing reimbursement policies at both the federal and state levels and rising medical costs that were headed toward the 17.9 percent of GDP it represents today. Above all else, the boards believed that the quality of care would not only be defended but enhanced by the strength of the merged institution to recruit the best doctors and medical professionals from all over the world.

The history of recent hospital mergers wasn't encouraging. In Massachusetts, Brigham and Women's Hospital and Massachusetts General Hospital had formed Partners HealthCare in 1994, signaling a trend but representing something short of a full merger. The 1997 merger of Stanford Medical and University of California San Francisco Medical in the California Bay Area ended in divorce. Mount Sinai and New York University Medical Centers announced their merger, but it fell apart in 1997 over control of the medical schools and other issues. We were four experienced CEOs, but managing the politics of such an amalgamation fully tested our capabilities. In our favor: unwavering focus on the urgency of a successful outcome for the benefit of patients and the communities served. The process—hard but good-faith bargaining and vital compromises—was a textbook lesson in reaching agreement. In January 1998, a full merger was completed and announced.

On the day we concluded our negotiations we gathered at John

Mack's golf club to celebrate. It may have been the effects of rain forcing our gathering indoors and a second glass of champagne doing the talking, but we agreed that despite our pride in our respective business successes, this effort on behalf of the literally millions who would receive medical care of the highest quality may have been the best thing we ever did.

Seldom, if ever, have I been exposed to such an enlightened and nonpartisan approach to a public good as exhibited by this group of true leaders. John McGillicuddy and Dan Burke have passed away, but my admiration for them, and my appreciation for what they did, remains unlimited. John Mack, who skillfully chaired the merged hospital for more than a decade, is among the executives I most admire and, more importantly, is among my most highly valued friends.

The results over twenty years have been remarkably good. Merging New York Hospital and Columbia Presbyterian Hospital brought together a combined board of trustees that I have often described as the best of any nonprofit board that ever existed. Skill and experience in every area of human activity resides within the membership of the board, and virtually every board member considers the NYP board the most important of his or her nonprofit associations.

John Mack, as the first chairman of the merged hospital, urged me to succeed him long before I found that possible. Not until I turned over the reins at Hearst to Steve Swartz could I say yes to that generous invitation. On January 1, 2014, I proudly became chairman of the board of trustees, a position I held until December 31, 2018. Jerry Speyer, a thoroughly experienced and greatly admired NYP board member, succeeded me as chairman. He will provide solid leadership for the next chapter in the life of this great institution. Hearst now has additional representation: Steve Swartz has established himself as an influential and effective hospital trustee, co-chairing the important Finance and Budget Committee.

The numbers say it all about the scale and quality of the health care delivered by NYP: Each year, more than 30,000 NYP professionals deliver care to more than 2,000,000 patients. Take that snapshot, multiply those numbers over two decades, and you get a sense of the significance of the merger.

My personal contributions feel modest, but they come with a sense of pride and ownership. Over my forty years as a trustee I've been privileged to serve on the search committees for three of the four physician CEOs to lead the organization. All have been doctors of high professional skills and extraordinary integrity and commitment. Dr. David Thompson was in place as The New York Hospital's CEO when I arrived, but I helped select Dr. David Skinner, who played a truly herculean role in the merger, Dr. Herbert Pardes, Columbia dean and health care leader of international reputation, who served as CEO of the merged enterprise for more than eleven years, and Steven J. Corwin, who in 2011, after twenty-five years of service in various roles within the institution, advanced to the CEO chair he fills now with such competence and dedication.

There have been surprises and bumps along the way. When John Mack and I and the search committee we chaired together had screened and/or interviewed a wide range of candidates who might succeed David Skinner, we woke up to the reality that we already knew the perfect candidate: Dr. Pardes, then dean of the

Columbia University College of Physicians & Surgeons. Some members of the Cornell community feared such a move could constitute a "Columbia takeover" at a fragile time when we were all working hard to ensure equal treatment and support of both of the merger partners. I went to see Dr. Tony Gotto, then dean of Weill Cornell, who praised Dr. Pardes as an inspired choice and pledged to make his full support known to the Weill Cornell faculty. Similarly, I went to see Sanford Weill, a longtime friend and former medical center fundraising partner of mine, who was then chairman of the Board of Overseers of Weill Cornell Medical College. Sandy echoed Dean Gotto's evaluation and used his substantial influence to support Dr. Pardes with the Overseers and Cornell Board. It was about this time that the fabulous gift from Sandy and his wife, Joan, another pal of mine, resulted in Cornell Medical becoming Weill Cornell Medical. I don't think after that anyone at either medical center gave any serious thought to Dr. Pardes's Columbia origin; he gave inspiring and immensely successful leadership to NewYork-Presbyterian.

Not only did the professional leadership come together, the two boards of trustees merged in remarkable style. I've often compared the ecumenical union of the boards to a story told by the late Bob Considine, a Hearst hero of bygone years. He was, he said, the father of two sons. One was adopted, "but for the life of me I can't ever remember which one." Today it's almost impossible to remember which board members came from legacy New York Hospital and which came from legacy Columbia Presbyterian. About a third joined after the merger.

That board and the superb leadership of CEO Dr. Steven Corwin, COO Dr. Laura Forese, and their gifted staff oversaw a

67 percent increase in NYP's net assets, an increase in a capital investment plan—already several billion dollars—by an additional $1.1 billion, and raised $1 billion in philanthropic support during the five years on my watch. The state-of-the-art David H. Koch Building was authorized and built. "Profits," although they aren't truly profits because they are entirely reinvested in medical advances and facilities—let's describe it as the hospital's black bottom line—grew steadily during the 2014–2018 period.

It is my fond hope that the five years I spent as chairman of Lincoln Center and subsequently a similar period as chairman of NewYork-Presbyterian, and my much longer board service to both institutions, will have resulted in leaving each of them in a better place than I found them. Which is not to say goodbye to either. As the bona fide flunked retiree I have demonstrated myself to be, I'm not going anywhere.

CHAPTER 18

Leave Something on the Table

If anyone knows that change is the law of life, I'm that man. I've been in a management role, primarily in media, through virtually every post–World War II recession. I've observed that radio didn't kill newspapers and magazines, as predicted. Nor did television kill radio, or newspapers and magazines. Nor did cable bring an end to television, radio, newspapers, and magazines. What's different now is velocity: so much change, hitting us at warp speed, that it's tempting to jettison much of what we know, lest we risk drowning. Plato, Shakespeare, Grand Opera, the wisdom of parents, teachers, and mentors? Abandoned by some, often in an instant.

But there is a paradox here. Just as there is no bigger or more dangerous trap than nostalgia, there is no better guide to a successful professional career and personal life than an understanding and appreciation of the past. Finding balance is a challenge no matter where you are in your life or career, but it's much more difficult when you are in charge. People not only look up to you, but rely on you to show them the way. They hope that your insights about the future will be on target and that the enterprise you share will reach its goals and their livelihood will be secure.

I often think about the all-hands meetings I held years ago at Hearst as we stuck our toe into the new waters known as the Internet. I was passionately urging the development of websites for our every business, predicting that the web would be more critical for us than the telephone. A veteran editor, standing in the back of the room, proclaimed for all to hear: "Thank God I'm old!"

In my business, even some of the brightest people seem to believe the future will obliterate the past. Witness two guys of uncontested brilliance who long ago earned my admiration. I remember Ted Turner, decades ago, saying that there will be no newspapers by the turn of the millennium; they'll all be gone. John Malone, some years ago, was asked about the future of local television stations. "They're toast," he said.

Those opinions are not baseless. It was my sad duty to stand in the offices of the *San Antonio Light* in 1992 and tell hundreds of the newspaper's employees that the newspaper would be put up for sale; if we couldn't find a buyer, the *Light* would be shut down. My New York colleagues didn't think it necessary that I personally deliver that news. I had no choice. This was the newspaper where my career had begun; this was the city of my birth. Only twenty years ago I had walked the halls of this paper as publisher. This would be the worst of days; it would have been easier to be announcing the closing of my high school.

But there are economic realities that now mandate one newspaper to a market—most often the morning newspaper—and those realities force days like that to occur all over the country. I told my San Antonio colleagues that we'd done everything possible to avoid this outcome, that many would find jobs at the surviving *San Antonio Express-News*, and that we would work hard to place those who did not. The reactions were mixed, but I believe the fact that I didn't hide out in my New York office was duly noticed and respected. In any event, it kept me from feeling even worse on a singularly sad day.

We know we must let the past go, and yet there's something to be said for continuity, for tradition, for the sheer pleasure of doing something you've "always done." I read on my iPhone and iPad, but I do that primarily when I travel. When possible, I still prefer reading the paper—the paper paper—and real magazines. I began my romance with media at my father's side and as a paperboy. We were called "junior merchants" in those days, a term I haven't heard for years. My belief is that our society is the loser when the paper route is no longer the typical first job for boys and girls.

I never fell out of love with print, despite my having been the unrelenting architect of converting Hearst, a century-old print company, into a diversified media organization in which the majority of our media is electronic and the future will be greatly aided by business-to-business databases. I still savor the smell of ink as newspapers come off the press, and the beauty and crispness of the yet-to-be-opened newspaper package. One of the few things that drive me crazy is when my wife, an even more dedicated newspaper reader than I am, gets to the *Times* or *Journal* first and leaves me with a rumpled, imprecisely folded residue with some pages missing, or articles and ads that have been torn out. I'll be sad if newspapers go completely online—but I don't expect that to happen for as far into the future as the eye can see.

I have the same love for ink-on-paper magazines. For those of us who make magazines, they're art: a magazine's beautiful pictures are, for me, more glorious, more stunning than even HD television. "Art" isn't a word widely used to describe magazines today, but I feel strongly it can be accurately applied to the final product created by gifted writers, photographers, and, yes, the creative wizards at ad agencies.

My longest tenured predecessor, Dick Berlin, reportedly described the ideal magazine publishing proposition as "one perfectly printed copy for every advertiser." Never true, Dick, and certainly not in today's world. Gil Maurer, who is the most skilled magazine executive I've known, has seen the flight of advertising to digital media and still has faith—well, a realistic faith—in the future of magazines. When we finally make it to Mars, he says, we're certain to find two familiar sights: a cockroach and a magazine. I can't speak to the prediction about cockroaches, but my guess is that magazines will last that far into the future only if those who publish them maintain the quality of their content and the beauty of their physical presentations. The equation is straightforward: Publishers who produce a combination of the highest quality print and digital editions, and understand they have different characteristics, will, in my humble but experienced opinion, maintain an impressive level of success.

If Helen Gurley Brown and John Mack Carter were editing magazines today, the chances are that the products of their brilliance would not be enough to jump-start a new wave of growth and diversification at Hearst as they did thirty-plus years ago. Today our entertainment businesses, primarily our cable networks, are playing that role. But that's just today. Hearst now does something most Americans would never associate with the company that publishes *Cosmo*—we collect massive amounts of data and organize the information for professionals. If you go into CVS to fill a prescription, it's a Hearst company that tells the pharmacist whether you should be warned about drug interactions. If you get into a car accident, there's a 90 percent chance that a Hearst-owned business is doing the estimate of the cost to repair. Investors and issuers in the bond markets and the owners of corporate jets rely on Hearst-owned Fitch Ratings and CAMP Systems, respectively, for vital information. It is thrilling to write those sentences—to know that we provide essential services, that we serve clients across many categories. And more: to know that we make a profit by doing truly good work in meaningful ways, not because we have mastered financial engineering.

The bottom line? Some shareholders of publicly traded companies and some owners of privately held businesses may only look at the stock price or the balance sheet. But an enterprise is a living organism; the numbers only give us one picture of its health. They don't tell us about the source of those numbers—the people who do the work. Do they feel respected and encouraged? Do they have a sense of mission? Or do they want to leave you for the first shiny opportunity they see? Human capital is an intangible asset, impossible to measure. But the spirit of your colleagues, the buzz in the cafeteria, the offices that don't empty out at 5 p.m.—these can give you information that really matters, which is nothing less than a prediction of a company's future.

The leader is crucial here, but not in a way that makes for splashy media. I endorse the words of Lao Tzu: "A leader is best when people barely know he exists, not so good when people obey and acclaim him, worse when they despise him. Fail to honor people, they fail to honor you. But a good leader, who talks little, when his work is done, his aims fulfilled, they will say, 'We did this ourselves.'"

I'd like to think I helped build a platform on which a great many people got to say, "We did this ourselves."

In a digital age, when too many employers treat their people like seasonal help, it's easy to fall into the trap of Xs and Os and to think that business is a zero-sum game: You win or you lose. If you haven't been trapped in a cave, you know better—your victory doesn't require your opponent's annihilation. In every interchange, in every transaction, it's not just good manners, it's good business. You may want to play another day. Leave something on the table.

Acknowledgments

Because this book has two separate but interconnected plots, the story of my life and the story of the modern history of one of America's most fabled companies, the 132-year-old Hearst Corporation, this author finds acknowledgments especially risky. Apologies in advance for missing those who clearly should have been included.

In the body of the book I have recognized many individuals who have been central in the personal, business, and pro bono aspects of my long visit on this planet. There are literally hundreds more to whom I am grateful.

A small army of friends, business associates, and family members provided critical contributions to my work on the book. William R. Hearst III, today's chairman of the Board of Directors of Hearst Corporation, encouraged this effort beyond almost anyone else. Those who joined him in that encouragement include numerous kind souls who know me well and a large number who would fall into the broader category of acquaintances. Virginia Hearst Randt, another senior board colleague, provided a much valued critique of the first draft of the manuscript and also offered greatly appreciated support.

Acknowledgments

Credit is also due to Steve Swartz, my admired successor as Hearst CEO, and Gil Maurer, COO and a genuine partner during much of my tenure at the helm, for the assistance and encouragement they gave me as I wrote the book.

In her typical fashion, Debra Shriver, Hearst's senior vice president and chief communications officer, took charge of logistics and many of the other needs an author has. She didn't let my procrastination get in the way of her unrelenting commitment that a book would come out of this undertaking. Deb's colleagues, particularly Sheila O'Shea, Judith Bookbinder, and Paul Luthringer, displayed not only remarkable skills but exceptional patience with me. Alex Carlin, who took on many of Deb's duties in 2018, has enthusiastically responded to every request for assistance.

Jesse Kornbluth, who refers to himself as a recovering journalist who now writes books and movies, has been an indispensable collaborator. He gave me a rare access to his consequential experience in authoring books, writing for leading periodicals, and creating movie scripts. Although I have written most of the words you have read, Jesse's edits and his contribution of some of the most professionally written passages make the book better by some margin than it would have been without his deft touch and advice. He is also an unrivaled raconteur, and therefore, truly good company. Pulitzer Prize–winning journalist Michael Leary, retired editor of Hearst's *San Antonio Express-News*, backed up my fact-checking.

Gloria Nicolosi, Buffy Lim Schmidt, and Tomasina Delaney, my dedicated executive assistants, took on the extra work resulting from this effort in good humor and ensured that we didn't miss a beat in the regular work of our office.

Acknowledgments

Had Robert "Bob" Barnett, partner in the storied Washington law firm Williams & Connolly, not agreed to represent me I doubt the project would have been finished, or even undertaken. Bob and his able associate Emily Alden have a legion of "real" authors to support, but at all times they took care of my business. Their help and counsel were extraordinarily valuable and greatly appreciated.

Jonathan Karp and Sean Manning at Simon & Schuster have not only been delightful to work with from the start of the project, but their counsel and engagement have resulted in a better manuscript. Their support and optimism helped me remain committed and enthusiastic. It was particularly a pleasure to be reunited with Carolyn Reidy, Simon & Schuster president and CEO, who was my colleague at William Morrow and during her stint as president and publisher of Avon Books when both publishing houses were part of Hearst. Her interest in this project meant a lot to me.

The enthusiasm for my writing this book demonstrated by my wife and children helped keep me at the keyboard on the days when, as happens to all authors, I imagine, I was not sure I had another paragraph in me. Dr. Mary Lake Polan, my wife of fourteen years, herself a published author, was unreservedly supportive but quite restrained in her advice. It may be that she took special note of the story I tell in the book about President Jimmy Carter's advice: Never write a book with your wife.

The Hearst Property List

Entertainment & Syndication

Cable Television Networks &
  Services

A+E Networks
  (including A&E, HISTORY,
  Lifetime, LMN & FYI—50%
  owned by Hearst)

Canal Cosmopolitan Iberia, S.L.

Cosmopolitan Television Canada
  Company
  (46% owned by Hearst)

ESPN, Inc.
  (20% owned by Hearst)

VICE Media
  (A+E Networks is a 17.8%
  investor in VICE)

VICELAND
  (A+E Networks is a 50.1%
  investor in VICELAND)

Digital & Content

BAMTech, LLC
  (15% of direct-to-consumer
  sports business owned by
  Hearst)

Complex Networks
  (50% owned by Hearst)

Hearst Entertainment

iflix
  (less than 10% owned by Hearst)

Kobalt Music
  (less than 10% owned by Hearst)

NorthSouth Productions
  (50% owned by Hearst)

Newspaper Syndication &
  Merchandise Licensing

Cowles Syndicate

King Features Licensing

King Features Syndicate

North America Syndicate

Reed Brennan Media Associates

Fitch Group

Fitch Ratings

Credit Ratings

Research & Commentary

Fitch Solutions

Counterparty Risk Solution

Debt Markets Solutions
Macro Intelligence Solution
Fundamental Financial Data
Ratings Distribution
Fulcrum Financial Data
Fitch Connect

Fitch Learning
Professional Qualifications
Corporate Solutions
Public Courses
CQF Institute

Hearst Health
Operating Businesses
FDB (First Databank, Inc.)
FDB UK (First Databank UK Ltd.)
Zynx Health
MCG Health
Homecare Homebase
MedHOK

Equity Investments
M2Gen

Venture Investments
Artemis Health
Tonic Health
Welltok
Aver Inc.
Lightbeam Health Solutions

Hearst Television
WCVB-TV, Boston, MA
WMUR-TV, Manchester, NH

WMOR-TV, Tampa/St. Petersburg, FL
WESH-TV, Orlando, FL
WKCF-TV, Orlando, FL
KCRA-TV, Sacramento, CA
KQCA-TV, Sacramento, CA
WTAE-TV, Pittsburgh, PA
WBAL-TV, Baltimore, MD
KMBC-TV, Kansas City, MO
KCWE-TV, Kansas City, MO
WLWT-TV, Cincinnati, OH
WISN-TV, Milwaukee, WI
WPBF-TV, West Palm Beach, FL
WYFF-TV, Greenville/Spartanburg, SC
KOCO-TV, Oklahoma City, OK
WVTM-TV, Birmingham, AL
WGAL-TV, Lancaster/Harrisburg, PA
KOAT-TV, Albuquerque, NM
WXII-TV, Greensboro/High Point/ Winston-Salem, NC
WCWG-TV, Greensboro/High Point/Winston-Salem, NC
WLKY-TV, Louisville, KY
WDSU-TV, New Orleans, LA
KCCI-TV, Des Moines, IA
KETV, Omaha, NE
WMTW-TV, Portland/Auburn, ME
WPXT-TV, Portland/Auburn, ME
WJCL-TV, Savannah, GA
WAPT-TV, Jackson, MS
WPTZ-TV, Burlington, VT/ Plattsburgh, NY
WNNE-TV, Burlington, VT/ Plattsburgh, NY

KHBS-TV/KHOG-TV, Fort Smith/
   Fayetteville, AR
KSBW-TV, Monterey/Salinas, CA

Radio
WBAL-AM, Baltimore, MD
WIYY-FM, Baltimore, MD

Production & Syndication
Litton Entertainment
   (majority owned by Hearst)

Magazines
Airbnbmag
Bicycling
Car and Driver
Cosmopolitan
Country Living
ELLE
ELLE DECOR
Esquire
Food Network Magazine
Good Housekeeping
Harper's BAZAAR
HGTV Magazine
House Beautiful
Marie Claire
Men's Health
O, The Oprah Magazine
Popular Mechanics
Prevention
Redbook
Road & Track
Runner's World
Seventeen

The Pioneer Woman Magazine
Town & Country
VERANDA
Woman's Day
Women's Health

International Magazine Activities
Hearst Magazines International

China
Beijing Hearst Advertising Co. Ltd.
Hua Dao
Shanghai Next Idea Advertising Co.,
   Ltd.

France
Inter-Edi, S.A.
   (50% owned by Hearst)

Germany
Burda Hearst Publishing GmbH
   (50% owned by Hearst)
Motor Presse Hearst GmbH & Co.
   KG Verlagsgesellschaft
   (50% owned by Hearst)

Italy
Hearst Magazines Italia S.p.A.

Japan
Hearst Fujingaho Co., Ltd.

Mexico
Hearst Expansión S. de R.L. de C.V.
   (51% owned by Hearst)

Televisa México
    (50% owned by Hearst)

Netherlands
Hearst Magazines Netherlands B.V.

Russia
Fashion Press
    (50% owned by Hearst)
Hearst Shkulev Media
    (50% owned by Hearst)
InterMediaGroup
    (50% owned by Hearst)

Spain
Hearst España, S.L.

Switzerland
Hearst Digital SA

Taiwan
Hearst Magazines Taiwan

United Kingdom
Handbag.com Limited
Hearst UK Limited
The National Magazine Company
    Limited

Hearst Magazines UK
Best
Cosmopolitan
Country Living
ELLE

ELLE Decoration
Esquire
Good Housekeeping
Harper's BAZAAR
House Beautiful
Inside Soap
Men's Health
Metropolitan Home
Prima
Real People
Red
Runner's World
Town & Country
Women's Health

Marketing Services
CDS Global, Inc. (U.S.)
CDS Global Limited (U.K.)
CDS Global Pty Limited (Australia)
iCrossing
KUBRA

Publishing Services
PubWorX
    (50/50 joint venture with Condé
    Nast)

Other
Hearst Autos
Hearst Content Extensions, Hearst
    Books & eReader
Hearst Global Licensing & Brand
    Development
Hearst Media Solutions

The Hearst Property List

Websites (U.S. & U.K.)
Best Products
CR Fashion Book
Delish
Digital Spy
NetDoctor
Shondaland

Newspapers
Beaumont Enterprise (TX)
Connecticut Post (CT)
Edwardsville Intelligencer (IL)
Greenwich Time (CT)
Houston Chronicle (TX)
Huron Daily Tribune (MI)
Laredo Morning Times (TX)
Manistee News Advocate (MI)
Midland Daily News (MI)
Midland Reporter-Telegram (TX)
New Haven Register (CT)
Plainview Daily Herald (TX)
San Antonio Express-News (TX)
San Francisco Chronicle (CA)
Seattlepi.com (WA)
Stamford Advocate (CT)
The Courier, Conroe (TX)
The Journal-Courier (IL)
The Middletown Press (CT)
The News-Times, Danbury (CT)
The Norwalk Hour (CT)
The Pioneer, Big Rapids (MI)
The Register Citizen (CT)
The Telegraph, Alton (IL)
Times Union (NY)

Weekly Newspapers
Atascocita Observer (TX)
Benzie County Record Patriot (MI)
Canyon News (TX)
Conexión (TX)
Cypress Creek Mirror, Champions/
    Klein (TX)
Cypress Creek Mirror, Cypress/
    Cy-Fair (TX)
Darien News (CT)
Deer Park Broadcaster (TX)
East Montgomery County
    Observer (TX)
Examiner, Heights (TX)
Examiner, West University/River
    Oaks/Bellaire (TX)
Fairfield Citizen (CT)
Friendswood Journal (TX)
Hardin County News (TX)
Herald Review (MI)
Humble Observer (TX)
Jasper Newsboy (TX)
Kingwood Observer (TX)
La Voz de Houston (TX)
Lake Houston Observer (TX)
Local First (NY)
Local Values (NY)
Magnolia Potpourri (TX)
Memorial Examiner (TX)
Milford-Orange Bulletin (CT)
Muleshoe Journal (TX)
New Canaan Advertiser (CT)
New Canaan News (CT)
News Advocate (TX)

Northeast Herald (TX)
Pasadena Citizen (TX)
Pearland Journal (TX)
Post-Chronicle (CT)
San Antonio Light (TX)
Shoreline Times (CT)
Southside Reporter (TX)
Spring Observer (TX)
Sugar Land Sun (TX)
The Advertiser (NY)
The Bay Area Citizen (TX)
The Darien Times (CT)
The Dolphin of Groton (CT)
The Foothills Trader (CT)
The Greater New Milford Spectrum (CT)
The Katy Rancher (TX)
The Lake County Star (MI)
The Litchfield County Times (CT)
The Milford Mirror (CT)
The Ridgefield Press (CT)
The Shelton Herald (CT)
The Trumbull Times (CT)
The Wilton Bulletin (CT)
The Woodlands Villager (TX)
The Zapata Times (TX)
Tomball Potpourri (TX)
West Hartford News (CT)
Westport News (CT)
Wilton Villager (CT)

Hearst Connecticut Media Group
Connecticut Magazine
Passport Magazine
The Connecticut Bride

The Litchfield County Times Magazine

Media Services/Yellow Pages Publishers
Associated Publishing Company
LocalEdge
Pioneer Directory Services (PDS)

Investments
Nucleus Marketing Solutions
   (25% owned by Hearst)
Slickdeals
   (20% owned by Hearst)

Digital Marketing Agencies
46mile
Amuse Digital
Tower Digital Agency

Ventures
8i
Amino
Atzuche
BuzzFeed
Caavo
Cogito
Decision Engines
DroneBase
Drone Racing League
Flash Delivery
GeoPhy
Kujiale
LAIX
LiveSafe

MobiTV
otonomo
Pixvana
PowerToFly
Relationship Science
Science
Sharecare
Signal Media
Snappy
Spartan Race
Stylus
Systum
Tezign
The Look
Via
WideOrbit
Wyng
Yoka
Zcool

Real Estate & Other Operations
Hearst Realties
Hearst Service Center

Western Properties
5M Project
Hearst Forests, LLC
LA Herald-Examiner
   Redevelopment
San Francisco Realties
San Simeon Ranch Division
Sunical Land & Livestock Division

West Coast Realties
Western Lands, LLC
Wyntoon Estate, LLC
Wyntoon Timberlands, LLC

Other Assets
Floor Covering Weekly

Hearst Transportation
CAMP Systems International
   (96% owned by Hearst)
MOTOR Information Systems
Black Book (National Auto
   Research)
Canadian Black Book

Hearstlab
AptDeco
Beam
FreeWill
Gloss Genius
HiOperator
KitSplit
LiveSafe
Mogul
PowerToFly
Priori
strongDM
Time Study
Trench
Wellspace
Wellthy

Illustration Credits

Index

Index

About the Author

FRANK BENNACK is executive vice chairman and former CEO of Hearst, a leading global media, information, and services company with more than twenty thousand employees and 360-plus businesses. During Bennack's time as CEO, he directed the company through an unprecedented period of growth, from his first twenty-three-year tenure starting in 1979 and through his second five-year run as CEO ending in 2013 when he stepped down—increasing revenues fourteen times and growing earnings more than thirty times. He is also chairman of the company's Executive Committee, a director of Hearst, and a trustee of the Hearst Family Trust. In addition, he sits on a number of corporate committees and the Hearst Foundations Boards, where he has served for more than twenty-five years. Bennack is currently a director of Ralph Lauren Corporation. He is chairman of Hearst Magazines UK, a wholly owned subsidiary of Hearst. Bennack is also a governor and former chairman of NewYork-Presbyterian Hospital and its Healthcare System, a managing director of the Metropolitan Opera of New York, chairman emeritus of Lincoln Center for the Performing Arts, and chairman of The Paley Center for Media (formerly The Museum of Television & Radio).